Against Hate

Carolin Emcke

Against Hate

Translated by Tony Crawford

polity

First published in German as *Gegen den Hass* © S. Fischer Verlag GmbH, Frankfurt am Main, 2016

This English edition © Polity Press, 2019

The translation of this work was supported by a grant from the Goethe-Institut

Polity Press
65 Bridge Street
Cambridge CB2 1UR, UK

Polity Press
101 Station Landing
Suite 300
Medford, MA 02155, USA

ISBN-13: 978-1-5095-3195-0
ISBN-13: 978-1-5095-3196-7 (pb)

A catalogue record for this book is available from the British Library.

Library of Congress Cataloging-in-Publication Data
Names: Emcke, Carolin, 1967- author.
Title: Against hate / Carolin Emcke.
Other titles: Gegen den Hass. English
Description: Medford, MA : Polity Press, [2019] | Includes bibliographical references and index.
Identifiers: LCCN 2018028019 (print) | LCCN 2018036515 (ebook) | ISBN 9781509531981 (Epub) | ISBN 9781509531950 (hardback) | ISBN 9781509531967 (pbk.)
Subjects: LCSH: Hate. | Fanaticism. | Racism. | Nationalism. | Cultural pluralism. | Toleration.
Classification: LCC BF575.H3 (ebook) | LCC BF575.H3 E4313 2019 (print) | DDC 152.4--dc23
LC record available at https://lccn.loc.gov/2018028019

Typeset in 11on 13 Sabon by Fakenham Pre Press
Printed and bound in by CPI Group (UK) Ltd, Croydon
The publisher has used its best endeavours to ensure that the URLs for external websites referred to in this book are correct and active at the time of going to press. However, the publisher has no responsibility for the websites and can make no guarantee that a site will remain live or that the content is or will remain appropriate.

For further information on Polity, visit our website:
politybooks.com

For Martin Saar

'But if all justice begins with speech, all speech is not just.'

Jacques Derrida

'Observing carefully means taking apart.'

Herta Müller

Contents

Preface

I sink in deep mire,
where there is no standing:
I am come into deep waters,
where the floods overflow me.
I am weary of my crying:
my throat is dried:
mine eyes fail
while I wait for my God.
They that hate me without a cause
are more than the hairs of mine head.

Psalm 69, 2–4

Sometimes I wonder whether I should envy them. Sometimes I wonder how they do it: how they hate the way they do. How they can be so sure of themselves. Because the haters have to be at least that: sure. Otherwise they would not talk the way they do, hurt the way they do, kill the way they do. Otherwise they could not insult others, humiliate others, attack others the way they do. They have to be sure of themselves. Beyond all doubt. You cannot hate and be unsure about hating at the same time. If they doubted, they could not be so beside themselves. Hating requires absolute certainty. Any 'maybe' would be a disruption. Any 'possibly' would undermine their hatred, sap the energy they are channelling into it.

Hate is fuzzy. It is difficult to hate with precision. Precision would bring delicate nuance, attentive looking and listening; precision would bring that discernment that perceives individual persons, with all their diverse, contradictory qualities and propensities, as human beings. But once the sharp edges have been ground down, once individuals have been blotted out as individuals, then all that is left are indistinct groups to serve as targets of hatred; then they can hate to their hearts' content, and defame and disparage, rave and rage: *the* Jews, *the* women, *the* unbelievers, *the* Blacks, *the* lesbians, *the* refugees, *the* Muslims, or perhaps *the* United States, *the* politicians, *the* West, *the* police, *the* media, *the* intellectuals.[1] Hatred distorts the object of hatred to suit itself. It forms its object to fit.

Hatred is aimed upwards or downwards, but always along a vertical axis: against those 'at the top' or the 'lowest of the low'. It is always the categorically 'other' who is oppressing or threatening the hater's 'self'; the 'other' is fantasized as a supposedly dangerous force or a supposedly inferior pest – and the subsequent mistreatment or annihilation of the 'other' is revalued accordingly, not just as an *excusable* act, but as a *necessary* one. The 'other' is the person who can be disregarded or denounced, injured or killed, without fear of punishment.[2]

Those who experience this hatred first-hand, who are subjected to it in the street or online, in the evening or in broad daylight, who have to endure words that carry a whole history of contempt and abuse, those who receive these messages wishing them death, wishing them sexual violence, threatening them with it, those whose rights are only partially conceded, whose bodies or headwear are despised, who have to disguise themselves for fear of attack, those who cannot leave the house because there is a brutalized, violent mob in front of it, those whose schools or synagogues need police protection – all those whom hatred takes as its object cannot and will not get used to it.

Of course, this subtle repulsion of people perceived as different or foreign has always existed. It was not necessarily tangible as hatred. In West Germany, it was usually expressed more as a rejection wrapped up in social conventions. In recent years there has also been an increasingly voiced uneasiness, a feeling that perhaps tolerance has gone a bit too far, that perhaps those with different beliefs or a different appearance or different desires ought to be satisfied by now. There was the discreet but unmistakable reproach that a little silent contentment might be expected of the Jews or the homosexuals or the women; they are permitted quite a lot now, after all. As if there were a limit on equality. As if women or gays were equal up to a certain point, but no further. Completely equal? That would be going a bit far. That would mean they were ... *equal*.

This curious reproach of lacking humility went hand in hand, covertly, with self-praise for the tolerance shown so far. As if it were a special benefit to allow women to work at all – so why do they need equal pay to boot? As if it were praiseworthy that homosexuals are no longer locked up as criminals. A little gratitude for that would be in order about now. For homosexuals to love each other privately is all well and good, but why do they need to be publicly married?[3]

This two-faced tolerance has often been expressed towards Muslims in the notion that, while they are free to live here, they should avoid being religiously Muslim. Freedom of religion has been accepted primarily in regard to the Christian religion. And we have heard, more and more often over the years, that it is about time there was an end to the endless discussion of the Shoah. As if the remembrance of Auschwitz had a limited shelf life, like a pot of yogurt. As if reflecting on the crimes of Nazism was an item on an excursion programme, to be looked at once and then ticked off.

But something has changed in Germany. People now hate openly and without restraint. Sometimes with a smile on their faces, sometimes without, but, all too often, shamelessly. The threatening letters that used to be posted anonymously are now signed with the sender's name and address. Violent fantasies and hateful comments are often expressed online without the cover of nicknames. If anyone had asked me a few years ago whether I could imagine that people would use *that* kind of language again in German society, I would have thought it impossible. For public discourse to become so brutal again, for people to stir up such unbounded hatred against other human beings – that was unimaginable. It almost seems as though the traditional conventions of conversation have been turned upside down. As if the standards of social behaviour have been reversed: as if a person should be ashamed of showing respect as a simple and natural form of politeness, and proud of refusing others respect and spewing vulgarities and prejudices at the top of one's lungs.

I, in any case, do not think uninhibited shouting, slandering and insulting represents an advancement of civilization. I do not consider it a sign of progress that every inner baseness may be turned outwards just because exhibiting resentments is now supposed to have some public or even political relevance. Like many other people, I refuse to get used to it. I do not want to see the new, unbridled appetite for hatred becoming normal. Neither in Europe nor anywhere else.

The hatred that I will talk about in this book is neither individual nor random. It is not just some vague feeling that happens to burst out by accident or out of ostensible distress. This hatred is collective, and it is ideologically moulded. Hatred requires ready-made patterns into which it can be poured. The concepts in which humiliation is doled out, the chains of association and the images that organize hateful thinking and sorting, the filters of perception that categorize and condemn – all these need preparation. Hatred does not break out suddenly; it is cultivated. And all those who interpret it as a spontaneous or individual phenomenon are unwittingly helping to keep it fed.[4]

Yet the rise of aggressive populist parties and movements in Germany, and across Europe, is not the most disturbing development. There is still reason to hope that they will decay in time of their own accord, through individual hubris and reciprocal animosities, or simply through the shortage of personnel able to carry out professional political work. To say nothing of the doubtful viability of an anti-modernistic platform which rejects the social, economic and cultural reality of a globalized world. They will probably lose their appeal when they are compelled to engage in public debates in which they have to present their reasoning and respond to that of others, when they are called upon to give factual arguments on complex issues. They will probably also lose their special, ostensibly dissident aura when they are met with occasional agreement – where appropriate – on individual points. That will make criticism all the more effective on other points. And, not least, far-reaching economic programmes will probably be necessary to address the social discontent over growing inequality and the fear of poverty in old age in disadvantaged regions and cities.

What is much more threatening is the climate of fanaticism, at home and abroad. The vicious circle of increasingly fundamental rejection of people who believe in a different faith, or in none, or whose looks or whose loves are different from some supposed norm. The contempt for everything different, spreading and growing and ultimately harming everyone. Because we who are the targets of this hatred, or who bear witness against it, are all too often dismayed into silence: we allow ourselves to be intimidated; we don't know how we are supposed to confront this rage and terror; we feel defenceless and paralysed; we are speechless with horror. Because that, sadly, is one of the effects of hatred: it first upsets those who are subjected to it, robs them of their orientation and their confidence.

The only way to confront hatred is to refuse its invitation to adopt it ourselves. Those who answer hate with hate have already allowed it to deform them, already come closer to what the haters want them to be. Because hatred can only be contested with what the haters lack: careful observations, unstinting precise distinctions, and self-doubt. That means slowly breaking hatred down into its component parts, separating the momentary feeling of hatred from its ideological prerequisites, and observing how it arises and operates in a specific historical, regional, cultural context. That may seem meagre; the project may appear overly modest. It might be objected that that is no way to reach the real fanatics. And that may be so. But it would be a step forward if the sources that feed hatred, the structures that enable it, the mechanisms it obeys, were more clearly visible. It would be a step forward if the self-assurance of those who approve and applaud hatred were taken away. If those who prepare hatred by shaping its patterns of thought and perception had their negligent naiveté or their cynicism taken away. If the burden of justification were lifted from those who quietly and peacefully work where they are needed, and were placed instead on the people who despise them. If the people who spontaneously reach out to those in distress were no longer called upon to give their reasons, but rather the people who refuse to give that indispensable aid. If it were not the people who want open, humane coexistence who had to defend themselves, but those who want to undermine it.

Examining hatred and violence together with the structures that enable them also means making visible the justification that precedes them and the approval that comes after: hatred and violence cannot thrive without this contextual support. Examining the different sources from which hatred or violence is fed in a specific case means disproving the popular myth that hatred is something natural, something given. As if hatred were more authentic than respect. But hatred doesn't come out of nowhere: people make it. And violence doesn't come out of nowhere: people prepare it. The direction in which hatred and violence are discharged, whom they are aimed at, what inhibitions and restraints must first be broken down – all this is not a matter of chance, not simply given; it is channelled. And examining how hatred and violence function, instead of just condemning them, necessarily involves showing where something could have been *otherwise*, where someone could have made a *different* decision, where someone could have *intervened*, where someone could have *backed out*. Describing the exact processes of hatred and violence necessarily involves showing where they can be interrupted or undermined.

Examining hatred in all its phases, not just from the moment it bursts out in blind rage, opens up other options. Certain forms of hatred fall under the responsibility of police and prosecutors. But the forms of exclusion and inclusion, the nasty little techniques of discrimination in gestures and habits, practices and beliefs – these are the responsibility of everyone in a society. As a civil society, we are all responsible for taking away the haters' space to distort their object to fit. We cannot delegate that responsibility. To assist those who are threatened because of their different appearance, different beliefs or different loves is not much to ask. It is little things that can make the difference and open the social or discursive space to those who are being driven out of it. Perhaps the most important gesture in opposing hatred is not letting it isolate us. Not letting ourselves be pushed into silence, into the private sphere, into the protected space of our own safe zones or milieus. Perhaps the most important movement is the movement outwards from ourselves. Towards the others. To reopen the social and public spaces together with them.

Those who are left alone in their exposure to hatred feel what the lamenting voice expresses in the psalm quoted above: 'I sink in deep mire, where there is no standing.' They have no ground under their feet; they feel as if they are out of their depth and the water is welling up over them. We must not leave them alone; we must listen when they cry out. Not allow the flood of hatred to well up higher. Build a solid footing on which everyone can stand: that is what is necessary.

1

Visible, Invisible

'I am an invisible man. [...] That invisibility to which I
refer occurs because of a peculiar disposition of the eyes
of those with whom I come in contact.'

Ralph Ellison, *Invisible Man*

He is a man of flesh and bone. Not a ghost, not a
figure on a movie screen, but a being with a body that
occupies a certain space, casts a shadow, may stand in
the way or block the view, says the Black protagonist
of Ralph Ellison's famous 1952 novel *Invisible Man*. A
person who speaks, looks people in the eye – and yet
it's as if he were surrounded by distorting mirrors in
which those who come into contact with him see only
themselves, or his surroundings. Anything except him.
How can that be? Why is it that *white* people cannot
see him?

Their eyesight is not impaired. There's no physio-
logical explanation; it is an inner attitude in the observer
that blots the man out and makes him disappear. He
does not exist to other people. As if he were air, or an
inanimate object, a lamppost, at most something which

forces them to step around it, but nothing that merits any greeting, any acknowledgement, any attention. To be unseen, unrecognized, invisible to others is really the most existential form of disrespect.[1] The invisible, those who are not seen, are not included in any social 'we'. Their words are ignored, their gestures overlooked. Those who are invisible have no feelings, no needs, no rights.

The African American poet Claudia Rankine also tells about the experience of invisibility in her most recent book, *Citizen*. A Black boy is knocked down in the subway by a man who 'did not see him'. The man keeps going, doesn't help the boy up, doesn't apologize. As if no contact had occurred; as if no person had been in his path. Rankine writes: 'And you want it to stop, you want the child pushed to the ground to be seen, to be helped to his feet, to be brushed off by the person that did not see him, has never seen him, has perhaps never seen anyone who is not a reflection of himself.'[2]

You want it to stop. You want not just some people to be visible, not just those who reflect some image that someone invented and declared the norm; you want just being a person to be enough, no other qualities or characteristics to be required, for a person to be seen. You don't want the people who look a little different from the norm to be overlooked; you don't want there to be a norm at all for what is visible and what is invisible. You don't want people who deviate from the norm to be knocked down because they have a different skin colour or a different body, because they love differently or believe differently or hope differently from the majority whose image sets the norm. You want it to stop because it is an insult to everyone, not just to those who get overlooked and knocked down.

But where does it come from, this 'peculiar disposition of the eyes', as Ralph Ellison calls it? How do certain people become invisible to others? What emotions are conducive to this kind of seeing in which some people are visible and others are not? What ideas nurture this inner attitude that blots out or masks over others? Who or what forms this attitude? How does it spread? What historical narratives shape such distorting or selective visual regimes? How does the frame arise that dictates interpretative patterns in which certain people are invisible and insignificant, or perceived as threatening and dangerous?

And, most importantly, what are the consequences for the people who are no longer seen, no longer perceived as persons? What does it mean to them to be ignored or seen as something other than what they are? As foreigners, criminals, barbarians, sick people – as interchangeable members of a group, not as individuals with individual abilities and affinities, not as vulnerable beings with names and faces? To what degree does this social invisibility rob them of their sense of orientation, sap their ability to defend themselves?

Love

> 'Feelings do not believe in the reality principle.'
> Alexander Kluge, *Die Kunst, Unterschiede zu machen*
> ('The art of making distinctions')

'Fetch me that flower!' commands Oberon, the king of the fairies, as he sends his jester Puck in search of a magical aphrodisiac. The herb has an inescapable effect: a drop of its juice on the eyelids of a sleeping person causes them to fall madly in love with the first creature they see upon awakening. Because Puck is not exactly the wisest of fairies, and mistakenly administers the potion to other victims than those Oberon intended, the plot of *A Midsummer Night's Dream* develops wondrous entanglements. The most sorely afflicted are

Titania, the queen of the fairies, and the weaver Bottom. Puck enchants the unwitting Bottom, turning him into a creature with a huge donkey's head. The good-natured weaver does not notice his deformation and is surprised to see everyone suddenly running away from him. 'Bless thee, Bottom! Bless thee!' says his friend Quince when he sees Bottom's ugly figure, and tries to tell him as gently as possible what has happened: 'Thou art *translated*.' Bottom thinks his friends are playing a rude joke on him: 'I see their knavery: this is to make an ass of me; to fright me, if they could', he declares, and strolls away singing defiantly.

In this beastly transformation, Bottom comes upon Titania in the woods where Puck has applied the aphrodisiac to her eyelids while she slept. And the magic takes effect; no sooner does she see Bottom than she falls in love with him:

So is mine eye enthralled to thy shape;
And thy fair virtue's force, perforce, doth move me,
On the first view, to say, to swear, I love thee.

Nothing against donkeys, but – Titania, looking at a half-beast, is 'enthralled' and calls it 'fair'? How can that be? What does she fail to see, or see differently? Is it possible that Titania doesn't notice Bottom's giant donkey ears? His shaggy fur? His huge muzzle? Perhaps, although she is looking at Bottom, she doesn't see his exact outlines, his features. The creature appears to her as altogether 'fair': perhaps she is simply blotting out all those qualities and characteristics that do not fit that label. She is moved, stirred, smitten, and her euphoria seems to have shut down some of her cognitive functions. Or perhaps – another possibility – she *does* see his huge ears, his shaggy fur and his muzzle, but, under the influence of the love potion, she *appraises* these aspects of Bottom otherwise than she normally would. She sees the giant ears, but to her they suddenly seem enthralling and fair.

What the magic flower's juice does as a dramaturgical device in Shakespeare's play is something we are familiar with in our own lives: love (or lust) has a way of suddenly overwhelming us. It takes us completely by surprise and affects our whole being. It is entrancing; it drives us out of our senses. Yet Titania falls in love with Bottom not because he is the way he is, but only because he is the first being she sees on awakening. It is true that, in her enchanted state, she loves Bottom – what she sees in him really does look lovely to her – but, although she can even name reasons why she loves him, they are not the true source of her love. In the story of Titania's love for Bottom, Shakespeare is telling us about those emotional states in which the object of the emotion is not the same as its cause. A person who has slept badly and wakes up irritable seizes on the most insignificant thing as an opportunity to discharge their anger. The object of their wrath is probably the first person they happen to meet, a chance victim, assaulted out of the blue – who has done nothing to cause the anger in the first place. An emotion can in fact be *aroused* by something other than the thing or the creature at which it is *directed*. Although Bottom is the object of Titania's love, he is not the cause of it.

And there is another lesson hidden in this story: love, like other emotions, involves *active ways of seeing*. Titania's perception of Bottom, the object of her love, is not neutral, but brings with it an appraisal and a judgement: she thinks of him as 'fair', 'virtuous', 'enthralling', 'desirable'. The power of her infatuation prevents her from having any inappropriate – that is, unwanted – perceptions; the lover's vision renders invisible any unpleasant properties or habits of the beloved. Anything that might be adverse to her love, anything that might impede the lover's emotion and pleasure, is repressed – at least in the initial infatuation. In this way, the object of love is *made to fit* the emotion brought to it.

Many years ago, a young interpreter in Afghanistan explained to me why it is a good idea for parents to choose a bride for their son. After all, he argued gently but firmly, when you're in love, you're completely blind and in no position to judge whether the woman you adore really suits you. But experience teaches us that love is not a permanent form of mental derangement; eventually the magical effect of Shakespeare's herb wears off – and then what? Then it is better if your mother, with her sensible eye, has chosen a wife who is still a suitable partner for you after the bewilderment of love has lifted. My Afghan interpreter had never seen his wife without a veil until their wedding day, and never talked with her alone until their wedding night. Was he happy? Yes, very much so.[3]

There are different ways in which we can project our own perceptions onto someone. Love is just one of the feelings that make us blot out reality. The imperturbable self-absorption of being in love has a certain charm because it elevates the other person, grants them a benevolent bonus. Because the projection is to the loved one's *advantage*. Love delights us by its power to overcome all resistance, any obstacle that reality puts in its way. A person in love does not want to grapple with objections or doubts. A person in love does not want to give explanations. To lovers, it is as if any argument, any rational appeal to one specific quality or another, would diminish their love. Love is a kind of acknowledgement of the other that, oddly, does not require knowledge at all. It requires only that I ascribe to the beloved certain properties which I conceive as 'fair', 'virtuous', 'enthralling', 'desirable'.[4] Even if those properties are donkey's ears and shaggy fur.

Hope

'Vain and deceptive hopes are for the foolish.'
Ecclesiasticus 34

In the legend of Pandora as told by Hesiod, Zeus sends Pandora down to Earth with a box full of vices and evils as yet unknown to humanity. She must keep the container of terrors closed at all costs. But, driven by curiosity, Pandora lifts the lid and looks inside, and then Illness, Hunger and Woe slip out of the box and spread throughout the world. And when Pandora closes the box again, she overlooks Hope, still lying in the bottom of it. Evidently, Zeus counted Hope among the evils. Why? Is hope not a good thing? Something that gives us positive inspiration and motivates us to do good deeds? Is hope not indispensable, just as love is?

Certainly, but the hope referred to in the Pandora legend is not that which we could call a well-founded prognosis or an optimistic disposition. The latter kind of hope is desirable and necessary. The hope that Hesiod writes about, on the other hand, is the empty kind of hope that rests on illusory assumptions. People who hold that kind of hope suffer from a propensity to believe that what they wish for will come to pass. It is a kind of unfounded anticipation that simply ignores what is easily discernible. Immanuel Kant calls this the 'partiality of the scales of reason' – in other words, hope causes a bias.

A person who absolutely yearns for something to turn out well turns their eyes away from signs that might diminish their hope. Intentionally or unintentionally, they blot out and make invisible whatever might pose an obstacle to the scenario they long for. Whether in regard to military, economic or medical prospects, hope easily clouds our view of any details or clues that are unfavourable to our own assumptions. Such signs are unwelcome because they prompt us to revise our all-too-optimistic prognoses. They are also somehow annoying, putting the brakes on our optimistic momentum, on our wishful thinking. It takes effort to confront unpleasant, complicated, ambivalent reality.

When a friend assures us he is not addicted, we wish it might be true. We watch him drink, watch him adapt the rhythm of his encounters and friendships to the rhythm of addiction, watch the addiction alienate him more and more from himself – and yet we refuse to believe it. We hope we are wrong; we hope we are not seeing what we are seeing: a friend is ill and we are losing him. We hope he will get better, and at the same time we prevent him from doing so, because he could only begin to get better by looking at his addiction realistically.

Sometimes, instead of blotting out the dark omens of an unfavourable outcome, hope reinterprets them. It inserts them in a more favourable reading, one we find more pleasing because it promises a better ending. Perhaps the story is more pleasing because it demands less of us. Maybe one day our friend comes to his senses and admits his dependency: in the conversations that ensue, he assures us he has finally seen through all the mechanisms of his addiction. He analyses himself better than we ever could. And again we hope that everything will turn out all right. All the clues that might run counter to that hope, anything that might expose our expectations as unrealistic or naive, become invisible. Perhaps, on top of everything else, we dread a conflict. After all, who looks forward to telling a friend something he doesn't want to hear? Who wants to intervene and put the friendship in danger? And so the deceptive hope continues to blot out everything, although it ought to be obvious that someone is ill and destroying himself.

Worry

> Who falls into my possession
> Finds no succour in Creation,
> Darkness ever settles on him,
> No sun sets nor rises on him,
> Healthy though his outward senses,
> Gloom resides inside the fences,
> And of all the offered treasures
> He cannot possess the pleasures.
>
> Worry, in Johann Wolfgang von Goethe, *Faust*,
> Second Part

'Who falls into my possession finds no succour in creation': thus the allegorical figure of Worry introduces itself in Goethe's *Faust*. It is midnight, and 'four grey women' – Want, Distress, Debt and Worry – would haunt Faust in the palace, but the door is locked. Only Worry creeps inside through the keyhole. When Faust notices her, he tries to keep Worry away from him; he parries what she says:

> Be still! You shall not burden me!
> I will not hear such balderdash expounded.
> Begone! That evil litany
> Could leave a sharper wit than mine confounded.

Faust knows well the dangerous power of Worry, her way of transforming even ordinary days into a 'nasty jumble', of making all possessions and all happiness appear worthless, and casting a gloomy veil over all favourable prospects. But much as Faust tries, Worry will not be banished. Before she finally does go, she breathes on Faust – and he is *blinded*.

Worry, as Goethe portrays it, takes possession of a person from inside. Losing his eyesight, Faust loses contact with the outside world. He no longer 'sees' anything but the demons that embitter his life by making everything appear dubious, threatening, awkward. While Hope blots out whatever contradicts its optimistic expectations, Worry denies everything that might dispel its fearful presentiments.

Of course, there are also justified forms of worry, better called care: these have to do with consideration, with mindfulness, with *caring for* others. But here we are concerned with that worry which feeds on itself and denies what we should be seeing and acknowledging. Worry admits no questions; it blots out anything that would cast doubt upon it. But care and worry, like love and hope, direct our attention to something in the world: in this case, something that is perceived as a (supposed) reason to worry. Just as Titania is able to give reasons why she loves Bottom, although Bottom himself is not the cause of her love, likewise worry can point to something that is no cause for worry. The object of worry is not necessarily the same thing as its cause. And the object of worry is sometimes *shaped to fit* the worry.

A person who thinks the Earth is flat may be terribly worried about *falling off*. And such a worry about falling into the abyss can be rationally justified: if the world is flat, then it has an edge, and if you go over the edge, you can fall off. It is completely rational to associate the edge with an abyss – and to be afraid of it. Those who worry because they think the world is flat cannot comprehend how others can be so calm, how they can go on living in their illusory serenity, as if the danger of falling into the abyss did not exist. Those who worry that anyone could fall off the edge do not understand why more isn't done to combat this danger. They despair at the deluded, clueless politicians who take no action to protect their constituents, who refuse to establish safety zones around the abyss, or who go so far as to claim there is no abyss in sight. That is all perfectly logical and consistent. Except that the Earth *is not* flat.

Maybe the cause – the thing that really is a reason to worry – is too big or too vague to be apprehended. Maybe the thing that makes a person worry can't be *grasped* exactly, because it instils such fear, and the fear is paralysing. Then worry picks out a different, more manageable object, something it can focus on, something which is not paralysing, but allows the person to take action. For a moment at least. For that brief moment, the person is then able to shut out the threatening, frightening phenomena, or to replace them with others that are easier to combat.

Worry is currently booming. Recent expressions of worry, the political rhetoric suggests, articulate a justified anxiety, an affect which we should take seriously, and must not criticize by any means. As if unfiltered feelings were justified by definition. As if unreflected feelings had a special legitimacy all their own. As if feelings not only must be felt, but always required uninhibited exposure and public expression too. As if all weighing and reflecting, all forms of scepticism towards one's own feelings or beliefs, constituted an unacceptable restriction on the satisfaction of one's needs. This rhetoric raises worry to a political category of peculiar authority.

There are, of course, social, political and economic concerns which ought to be publicly debated. There are, of course, understandable reasons why people who are more unprotected, more vulnerable, more marginalized than others worry about growing social inequality, about their children's uncertain opportunities for advancement, about the lack of funds in municipal coffers or the accumulating neglect of public institutions. And there are, of course, legitimate questions as to how and where to express one's political or social doubts and hardships. I certainly share some of the concerns about the political reaction to immigration: How to prevent the short-sighted housing policy of building quick and cheap high-density projects today in remote areas which will be deplored tomorrow as cultural and social slums? How to shape an education policy that addresses not only the young men who are needed in the labour market, but also their mothers, who should have a command of the language in which their children and grandchildren will grow up, the language of the government agencies, of the world around them? How to protect refugees against the spreading racism and violence, and how to prevent the formation of a hierarchy of suffering or poverty between different marginalized groups? How to shape a culture of remembrance without turning it into an ethnic history that excludes others? How to open and expand our narration of the past without losing our relation to the Shoah? I am no more qualified than anyone else to judge the necessity of all these concerns. But they can be publicly discussed and subjected to rational criticism.

The concept of the 'concerned citizen', on the other hand, functions nowadays as a discursive shield intended to deflect questions about the rational reasons for worries. As if worrying were in itself a compelling argument in a public discourse, and not merely an affect that can be justified or unjustified, appropriate or inappropriate, reasonable or exaggerated. As if we could not ask in regard to worry, just as we can in regard to love or hope, what it refers to, what elicits it, and whether its cause and its object are the same or two different things. As if worry did not have that power that Goethe speaks of in *Faust*, obscuring the vision of those whom it captures, blinding them to all that is stable and secure, all happiness and prosperity.

There is no reason to disparage the people who worry. But they must allow the concern they present to be closely examined and analysed into its components.

Those who worry must tolerate a distinction between a concern and what the philosopher Martha Nussbaum calls 'projective disgust' – that is, the rejection of other people on the pretext of self-protection.[5] There are many affective forces which undermine the social will to empathy, and which are in fact distinct from concern. For Nussbaum, one of these forces, along with fear and projective disgust, is narcissism.

The people who talk now about 'concerned citizens' primarily want to portray them in isolation from anything that could be subjected to political or moral criticism. Most importantly, they suppose 'concerned citizens' to be something other than racists or right-wing extremists. No one wants to be a racist. Not even the racist wants to be a racist, because the label, at least, is still socially taboo. That is why the feeling called 'concern' is useful as camouflage. Worry cloaks the hostility to others that it sometimes harbours, and offers protection against all criticism. Thus the taboo is both fulfilled and subverted simultaneously: the social rejection of xenophobia is affirmed, but at the same time challenged. What is presented as concern shifts the threshold of what is acceptable because it contains disgust, resentment and contempt.

The 'concerned citizens' may hate immigrants; they may vilify Muslims; they may abhor and disdain people who look differently, love differently, believe differently or think differently than they do – but all these beliefs and affects are concealed by their supposedly unassailable worry. The concept of the 'concerned citizen' suggests that they are sacrosanct. After all, what could be morally reprehensible about their concern? As if a society must permit everything; as if there must be no norms of acceptability or unacceptability, because any norm would restrict the free egocentrism of the individual.

The term 'concerned citizen' is no longer used only by people who hide behind it – such as the supporters of the new political organizations in Germany, PEGIDA (an association calling itself 'patriotic Europeans against the Islamization of the West') and the AfD (the 'Alternative for Germany', founded in 2013 as a Eurosceptic party). Now certain journalists are also contributing to this strange glorification of emotions, when they should be calmly and precisely analysing the causes and the objects of the people's worries, justifying their concerns where there is justification for them, and criticizing them where they have no real, factual foundation. The journalist's duty is not to agree with whatever his or her readers think, not to give sympathetic coverage to all social movements per se, big or small, but to analyse their arguments, their strategies and methods, and to examine them critically where necessary.

It is necessary, certainly, to consider whether this hatred shrouded in 'concern' might be a place-holder (or an outlet) for collective experiences of disenfranchisement, marginalization or a lack of political representation. The question calls for a level-headed investigation of its causes, of the sources of the energy that is now being discharged in hatred and violence in so many places. The societies concerned may also ask themselves critically why they were not able to recognize earlier the injuries to which hatred and identitarian fanaticism are only a misguided reaction. What ideological blinds prevent the perception of a resentment of social inequality?

The most promising examination of this question seems to me to be Didier Eribon's reasoning – building on Jean-Paul Sartre – that those groups and milieus which are formed by negative experiences are especially inclined towards fanaticism and racism. According to Sartre's analysis, certain groups, which he called 'series', are formed through passive, unreflected processes of adaptation to a restrictive, resistant environment. Thus what bonds such series together is the feeling of helplessness in the face of a social reality – and not a feeling of active, self-assured identification with a purpose or an idea.[6] Eribon specifically examines the inclination of the French working class to support the *Front national*. But other contexts and milieus may also offer fertile ground for a structural analysis of the origins of groups and movements that, rather than crystallizing around a conscious political intention, are more strongly moulded by materially negative experiences (or objects). As the motivation of a community, racism or fanaticism usurps the place of what might really unite the individuals: 'it is the absence of political organization, or the absence of the perception that one belongs to an organized social group, that makes it possible for a racist form of division to replace a division based on class'.[7]

According to this interpretation, it is necessary first to penetrate the racist and nationalist patterns (and thus to protect those subjected to them) in order to reveal the social issues that have been neglected or blocked out. Perhaps this is the special tragic quality of fanatical and illiberal dogmatists: that they fail to address precisely those issues that are valid causes of political concern. 'The treacherous thing about worry is that it stands in the way of a solution to the problem by pretending to seek one.'[8]

Hatred and Contempt, Part 1: Group-focused Hostility (Clausnitz, Saxony)

'Monstrosity and invisibility are two subspecies of the other.'

Elaine Scarry, 'The Difficulty of
Imagining Other Persons'

What do they see? What do they see differently from me? The video is short – maybe too short. You can watch it again and again and still not understand it. Darkness frames the scene like a cloak; the central light source is the greenish-yellow inscription *Reisegenuss*, 'travelling pleasure'; to the left of it, something yellow and rectangular, probably the side mirror of the coach. In the foreground, only the backs of people's heads are visible as they stand outside gesturing towards the passengers on the coach, their thumbs up, index fingers forward, chanting loudly, '*Wir sind das Volk*', 'we are the people'. At no point in the video do we see them from the front. They are present only as moving hands, as a collective slogan, as if that slogan explained itself, or their hatred for others. 'We are the people': a historic quotation from the peaceful uprising of East Germans against the communist regime, the slogan means in this moment, in this town in Saxony, 'And you're not.' It means, 'We are the ones who decide who belongs and who doesn't.'[9]

What, or whom, do they see in front of them?

The camera zooms slightly towards the windscreen of the coach; seven figures can be seen standing or sitting inside at the front: on the right a driver, impassive, a baseball cap pulled down low over his face; in the front seat on the left two younger women; in the aisle two men, their backs turned to the howling crowd outside, apparently exhorting the paralysed refugees in the coach. One of the men has his arms around a child: we see only two small hands clutching his back.

How long have they been sitting there? How long has their coach been blocked? Has anyone talked to the people standing there shouting and keeping it from driving on? The images give no answers. An older woman with a beige headscarf standing in the aisle looks at the shouting crowd in front of the coach, clearly upset; she gesticulates towards the people screaming at her and spits – or at least makes a spitting gesture. As the crowd's chant of 'We are the people' signals 'You are outsiders', 'You don't belong', 'You can get lost', her spitting signals a 'No': 'No, we do not deserve this humiliation.' 'No, that is no way to behave.' 'No; what kind of people are they claiming to be, to make such a spectacle of themselves?'[10]

Then the child is released from the protective embrace, and we see for the first time a boy in a blue hooded jacket, his face contorted, evidently crying: he looks towards the crowd whose slogans he doesn't understand, but whose gestures are unmistakable. He is supposed to go out there. The boy is led through the door of the coach into the dark, where the crowd is now yelling, 'Go away ... go away.' Inside we can now see the two women in the front seat, holding each other, one hiding her face on the other's shoulder while the other wipes tears from her eyes.

Those people standing outside shouting – what do they see? The video from Clausnitz has been debated and commented on at length. Almost everyone who saw it was shocked and outraged. They called it a 'disgrace', they called the crowd a 'mob', and most of them try, in speech or writing, to dissociate themselves from the scene. At first, I was amazed. My first response, before horror, was incomprehension. How is this *possible*? How is it possible to see the crying child, the two frightened young women in the front seats of the coach – and scream 'Go away'? The protesters are looking at frightened human beings, and they see neither fear nor human beings. What techniques of blinding or blotting out does it take to do that? What ideological, emotional, psychological circumstances can so shape their perception that they do not see people as human beings?

In Clausnitz, people are not merely made invisible – the refugees in the coach are not simply overlooked like the boy in the subway in Claudia Rankine's text – they are not ignored; they are perceived as something detestable.

'Hatred requires taking the object of hatred seriously',
Aurel Kolnai wrote in his analysis of hostile feelings. 'It
must be in some way important, significant, dangerous,
powerful.'[11] In this light, the slogan 'We are the people'
does not go far enough. Hatred means more than just
that these people supposedly belong here and those do
not. That would be too trivial. Then the new arrivals
could be simply dismissed as irrelevant. Then 'the people'
could have stayed home on the evening the refugees
arrived. They could have turned their attention to more
important things. Something else is happening here.

First, the refugees in the coach are being made
invisible as individual persons. They are not seen as part
of a universal 'we'. They are being negated as human
beings with individual histories, individual experiences
and qualities. And, at the same time, they are being
made *visible*, or construed, as others, as 'not us'.
Qualities are being projected onto them to shape and
mark them as a strange, repulsive, dangerous group.
'Monstrosity and invisibility are two subspecies of the
other,' Elaine Scarry writes, 'the one overly visible and
repelling attention, the other unavailable for attention
and hence absent from the outset.'[12]

Hatred is happening in this scene from Clausnitz,
and in hatred, the object of hatred must be thought of
as critically important and monstrous. That presup-
poses a wilful reversal of the actual relation of power.
Although the new arrivals are quite obviously powerless
– although they have no property other than what
has survived their trek in a plastic bag or a rucksack,
although they speak no language in which they could
express or defend themselves here, although they have
no home any more – they must be conceived as a
powerful threat against which the supposedly helpless
'people' must take a stand.

In this video, three groups of persons can be seen
standing around the coach: first, those chanting and

shouting; second, those watching them; and third, the police.

First: Little is known even today about the men chanting in front of the coach. They are a diffuse group, variously designated as a 'mob', a 'rabble', a 'horde'. I do not care for any of these terms. I have no interest in condemning these people as human beings.[13] We do not know their age or their educational level; we know nothing about their social or religious background, nor whether they have jobs or are unemployed, nor whether they have ever encountered refugees in their region before. I am not so much interested here in the biographies of the haters. I am not so much interested in whether they would individually identify themselves as 'right-wing', whether they are affiliated with a political organization or party, whether they support the AfD or the communists' successor party *Die Linke*, whether their musical tastes run to white power metal, gangsta rap, or German pop. The Saxon police would later report only that a group of about one hundred people, most of them from the area, protested in front of the refugee shelter in Clausnitz.

What I am interested in is what these people say and what they do; I am interested in their *actions* – and, accordingly, I will designate them in the pages that follow as people who hate, who shout, who protest, who defame. Examining and criticizing actions – not persons – leaves open the possibility that the persons can renounce their actions, that they can change. In this perspective, I am not judging a person or a whole group; I judge what they say and do in a *specific* situation, and the harm they cause. This perspective admits that these persons could also act otherwise in another situation. Thus, what interests me are the following questions: What enables them to perform this act? Where does this language come from? What is the background of this act? What interpretative patterns does this view of refugees presuppose?

On the Facebook page where the short video from Clausnitz was apparently first posted, 'Döbeln Fights Back: Speak Out Against the Flood of Immigration',[14] it appears as the climax of a sequence of eleven photos with numerous comments referring to the transport of refugees.[15] There is no indication who took the pictures or when. They seem to show a number of different coaches, documenting their trips to or from refugee shelters. The series begins with a photo showing a dark scene: in the middle is a deserted road, apparently situated in an industrial zone; two buildings project into the frame at the left edge, and the back half of a white bus is seen turning left around the corner of one of the buildings. The photo is captioned 'On the Quiet in Döbeln', followed by the comment: 'Shortly after 6:00 at Autoliv. They're bringing the new specialists in robbery and theft.'

'Autoliv' refers to a Swedish manufacturer of safety equipment which had closed down its production site in Döbeln two years previously. From 1991 on, Autoliv had produced seat belts, buckles and height adjusters in Döbeln. The company first cut back the original staff of 500 employees to 246, then closed the Döbeln works in 2014 and moved its production to Eastern Europe.[16] In late 2015, after negotiations with the owner of the site, the vacant factory building was turned into a receiving centre with space for up to 400 refugees. What an arbitrary redirection: because there is no addressee on hand for the people's anger at the company, they now aim their anger at those who fill the site vacated by the original addressee? The target of the people's wrath is not those who closed down the factory, but those who need the vacant building? It is not the executives of Autoliv who are slandered as 'specialists in robbery and theft', but the refugees who are assigned to stay in the redundant buildings?

Another photo shows only the rear of a coach, painted with the legend *ReiseGenuss pur*: 'pure travelling pleasure'. That is the brand name of a regional tour operator whose website explains what is meant by such 'pleasure': 'Spend your holiday in cheerful company, join old acquaintances or meet nice people.' Other photos in the sequence show some of the nice people the refugees were able to meet with *ReiseGenuss* on 18 February, 2016: in one picture, a car is stopped diagonally in front of a coach, evidently blocking its way.[17] Another picture shows a tractor with a banner tied across its shovel: 'Our Country – Our Rules: Homeland – Freedom – Tradition', which is funny in a way, since neither 'homeland' nor 'freedom' nor 'tradition' suggests a single rule that could be derived from it. Furthermore, there is a possible contradiction at least between 'freedom' and 'tradition' which is not resolved.

The photo series frames the video in the story of a kind of chase, as if a coach full of refugees had been hunted like an animal and finally brought to bay. The story is quite obviously not unpleasant to the Facebook page's administrators and contributors, otherwise they would not document and publish it in this way; it is the story of a kind of hunt which the participants feel justified in carrying out. They have no doubt whatever about their activities, which involve blocking a coach for more than two hours and intimidating and threatening children and women. On the contrary, the hunting party present themselves at the conclusion of this story as both angry and proud in front of their helpless quarry.

What makes the genre of the chase and the blockade so interesting is the desire to get close to what is ostensibly dangerous. The vehicles pictured are different coaches – the one in the first photo, from Döbeln, is not the one blocked in Clausnitz – but the scenes are linked by the series of photos decrying the transport of refugees ('On the Quiet in Döbeln'). It is not known with certainty when the blockaders began waiting for the coach in Clausnitz and who informed them that it was coming. What is certain is this: all the people who blocked the coach were evidently *seeking* a confrontation. The refugees were not being *avoided* by the people who allegedly feared them; the refugees did not elicit abhorrence or repulsion; on the contrary, they were being sought after and cornered. If fear or worry had been the protesters' critical motivation (as has often been claimed), they would not have sought to get *closer* to the refugees. A person who is afraid wants to put as much distance as possible between themselves and the danger. Hatred, on the other hand, cannot simply take a detour around its object or keep it at a distance: it needs its object within reach in order to be able to 'annihilate' it.[18]

Second: The second group around the coach in Clausnitz consists of the spectators. They are not filled with such hatred. There were probably people among them who were drawn simply by the thrill of a scandal, or the mere entertainment that any provocation brings with it, catapulting them out of the boredom of their day-to-day lives. There were probably tag-alongs too who did not shout, but only watched in awe as the others shouted. Who took a pornographic enjoyment in the others' abandonment of all inhibitions, rather than feeling they could be so uninhibited themselves. These participating non-participants are also visible in the video and photos. They stand surrounding the shouters, constituting a forum which lends them the attention they need to assert themselves as 'the people'.

The spectacular character of such performances gives them a double effect. The spectacle is aimed at an audience which grows as the provocation becomes more extraordinary. And, at the same time, the spectacle is aimed at the victims, who cannot escape becoming part of a theatrical performance that humiliates them. The spectacle not only frightens the victims, but also exposes them to an audience which degrades them to an object with entertainment value. The spectacle of a crowd has a history: the ostentatious public humiliation of marginalized people, the demonstration of power in an arena in which defenceless people are harried or lynched, their houses and their businesses damaged or destroyed; these are old, traditional techniques. The spectacle of Clausnitz takes its place in the history of all those spectacles that terrorize people of a given religion, a given skin colour, a given sexuality by demonstrating to them that they are not safe. That their bodies are vulnerable. At all times.

On watching the video over again, this surprises me more than the howling crowd right in front of the coach: what is this audience doing? Why doesn't anyone among the onlookers intervene? Why does no one talk to the men chanting slogans and try to calm them down? Why do the bystanders delegate their capacity for action to the police? They are neighbours, acquaintances, people of Clausnitz; they know each other from school, from work, from the street. Perhaps some of them are visitors from other towns, but many of them know each other. Why doesn't anyone step forward and say, 'Come on, that's enough now'? People are capable of that in any football squad. Why doesn't anyone try to say, 'Let's go'? Perhaps no one dares. Perhaps the mood is too aggressive. Maybe the crowd is too angry; maybe it's too dangerous to criticize them, or to speak to them at all.

But if that is the case, why do the spectators stay there? Why don't they go home? All those who remain in the audience only increase the size of the crowd confronting the people in the coach. All those who stand still and gawk serve as resonators amplifying the haters. Perhaps they didn't think of that. Perhaps they just wanted to watch, as if that were not also an act that affects others. Perhaps they felt uneasy only afterwards, when it was all over. In that case, this should give them something to think about after the fact: every single one of those who stand by watching could walk away, and by doing so give the signal, 'Not in my name.' Every single one of them could demonstrate: this is not my nation; this is not my language, not my gesture, not my attitude. That doesn't take much courage. It only requires a little decency.

Third: 'Rage is vented on those who are both conspicuous and unprotected', wrote Max Horkheimer and Theodor W. Adorno in the *Dialectic of Enlightenment*.[19] The police are the third actor in the video. At first, it is reassuring that they are there at all. No one knows what might have happened without the police on the scene. Whether the hatred might have escalated further into violence against the refugees. So it is a good thing, and important, that a force of order is present which can prevent violent assault. However, the officers on the scene in Clausnitz apparently have difficulty pacifying the situation. Why? We can only speculate as to the reasons. There are no recordings from inside the coach, so we cannot hear whether the officers may have tried to help the refugees. But little was heard about such efforts after the fact. The images merely show how long the police watched the activity of the screaming crowd, or in any event were unable to suppress it effectively. There are no megaphone announcements, as there usually are when blockades occur at demonstrations. No warning that names will be taken and the road forcibly cleared if the demonstrators fail to disperse. No such action can be seen here. The police seem mainly to have spoken to the passengers in the coach, as if it was the refugees who needed to be called to order, and not the agitators and their audience in front of the coach. In some photos, the onlookers can be clearly seen surrounding the bus without an officer keeping them away. A police operation like this, falling into some strange category between listless and helpless, signals to the blockaders by its demonstrative ambivalence that they can *go on*.

Of course, to the police's credit it must be mentioned that the situation also poses an objective problem: as long as the crowd is still in front of the coach shouting, the refugees will be terrified to leave the coach. But, instead of first pushing back the blockaders and then calmly encouraging the refugees to disembark together, the officers react resolutely and roughly only when the refugees in the coach begin to resist the situation. Rather than restraining the people who are preventing the coach from reaching the entrance of the refugee shelter, they constrain the people who are being intimidated and shouted at. When one of the boys in the coach shows his middle finger to 'the people' in front of the coach, a police officer drags him out of the vehicle by physical force, as if he were a criminal and not a child who has just spent more than two hours being insulted and threatened by a crowd of about a hundred people. Perhaps there were other officers who would have preferred to resolve the situation differently: more promptly, and with more consideration for the terrorized refugees. But if there were, they were apparently unable to assert themselves.

᙮

Nothing in the photo sequence indicates any wrongdoing on the part of the refugees. Nothing in the photo sequence, nor in the subsequent reporting, makes reference to any prior history that might explain why the passengers in the coach should be unwelcome; nothing in the photo sequence relates to the individuals in this coach at all. The hatred in this situation generates its force precisely by ignoring or going beyond the actual reality. No real reference, no real reason is necessary. Projection suffices. The hatred is aimed at these refugees

– it takes them for its object – but they are not the cause of it. Just as Titania loves Bottom not because he is what he is, but because the magic potion seduces her, the Clausnitz blockaders do not hate the refugees because they are what they are. Just as respect and acceptance presuppose the recognition of the other, the condition for contempt and hatred is often the failure to recognize the other. In hatred too, the cause of the emotion is not necessarily the same thing as its object. Just as Titania could give reasons why she loves Bottom, the haters of Clausnitz could also give reasons why they hate the refugees – and yet those reasons are not the reason for their hatred. They only ascribe to these refugees, as to all other refugees, certain properties, evaluating them as 'despicable', 'dangerous', 'abominable'.

But how did this hatred originate? Where does this view come from, this template in which refugees are perceived as 'despicable'?

Hatred doesn't arise out of nothing. Not in Clausnitz, Freital or Waldaschaff. Not in Toulouse, Paris or Orlando. Not in Ferguson, Staten Island or Waller County. *Hatred always has a specific context out of which it arises and in which it declares itself.* Someone has to *produce* the reasons that hatred appeals to, the reasons that are intended to explain why a group allegedly 'deserves' to be hated, in a specific historical and cultural context. The reasons have to be presented, narrated, illustrated, again and again, until they leave a residue in the form of dispositions. To continue the Shakespearean analogy: someone has to brew the potion that causes the affect. Hot, acute hatred is the consequence of cold practices and beliefs long prepared or handed down through generations. 'Collective dispositions of hatred and contempt [...] cannot subsist without the corresponding ideologies which represent the socially despised or hated persons as a social harm, a danger or a threat.'[20]

The ideology that leads to hatred in Clausnitz is not manufactured in Clausnitz alone. Nor is it manufactured in Saxony alone. It is manufactured in all those contexts – on the Internet, in discussion forums, in publications, on talk shows, in song lyrics – in which refugees are categorically never visible as equal human beings with their own dignity. To analyse hatred and violence we must examine these discourses in which the patterns and templates that prepare and justify hatred and violence are cut out.[21] Even the Facebook page 'Döbeln Fights Back', where the video from Clausnitz was first published, furnishes such preparation. It is not a forum with a particularly wide audience, but it contains all the templates of resentment and defamation that make the people in the coach invisible *as human beings* and visible *as a monstrosity*. This is just one example of the ideology which is found in countless other pages of radical right-wing organizations, PEGIDA-supporting groups and persons, and which could just as well be analysed using different examples.

The first thing that stands out is an intentionally *narrow* view of reality. There are no references, no information, no stories of migrants with a distinctive humour, musicality, technical skills, intellectual or artistic or emotional qualities. There are also no reports about the misfortunes, weaknesses or narrow-minded habits of individual migrants. In fact, there are no individuals at all. There are only stereotypes. Every single Muslim and every single Muslimah (although mainly male Muslims are implicated) is treated here as representing all Muslims. Which Muslim or migrant is instrumentalized for this purpose is arbitrary, as long as they can be used as examples to demonstrate the alleged wickedness of the whole group.

The world of the haters is like that of 'Crimewatch' – except that the cases have already been solved. The culprit is always Islam, always Muslim immigration,

always the criminal energy allegedly inherent in
every person who has fled his or her native country.
Society is in a permanent state of emergency, the
ideology suggests, in which there is no room for private
happiness, for all the odd, absurd, moving – perhaps
also annoying, tedious – experiences of living together.
In this world there simply is no normality. There are
only exaggerated exceptions that are purported to be
the norm. This world is purged of any real cultural,
social or even simply political diversity. There are no
harmless encounters, no satisfactory experiences, no
amusing occurrences. All ease, all pleasure is out of
place here.

What is the result of such a filtered view of the
world? What is the effect of perceiving people over and
over again only in a certain role, in a certain position,
with a certain attribute? At first, it doesn't even produce
hatred. This narrowed vision primarily cripples the
imagination. The worst thing about forums and publications in which refugees appear always and only as a
group and never as individuals, in which Muslims are
described always and only as terrorists or backward
'barbarians', is that they make it almost impossible
to *imagine* migrants as anything else. They narrow
the scope of the imagination, and with it the space
of empathy. They reduce the endless possible ways of
being Muslim or migrant to *one* form. And by doing
so, they link individual persons to groups, and they
link groups to the same invariable attributes. People
who get their information only from these media, who
are shown only this filtered view of the world and the
people in it, are constantly imprinted with the same
chains of association. With time, they become almost
unable to think of Muslims or migrants in any other
way. Their imagination is crippled. All that is left are
those mental abbreviations that reduce thinking to
ready-made attributions and judgements.

To understand this method of narrowing reality, just imagine a different variation of it: a Facebook page or a newspaper or a television programme which mentions Christians *only* when they have been convicted of a crime, and places every single crime committed by a Christian person in *causal* connection with their religion. A medium which never carries a single report about couples in love who are Christian, about Christian women solicitors specializing in tax law, about Catholic farmers or Protestant auto mechanics, no stories about sacred choir music or theatre festivals in which Christian actors perform – but only, exclusively, reports about the Ku Klux Klan, attacks by radical anti-abortion activists, and individual crimes from domestic violence to child abuse to kidnapping, armed robbery and murder – all of them, always, under the heading 'Christianity'. How would a template like that change people's perception?

'The human capacity to injure other people is very great', Elaine Scarry writes, 'precisely because our capacity to imagine other people is very small.'[22] When the imagination is so restricted, the capacity for empathy with a given person also shrinks. A person who can no longer *imagine* how unique, how individual, every single Muslimah, every single migrant, every transgender person or every Black person is, who cannot imagine how similar they are in their fundamental pursuit of happiness and dignity, is also unable to recognize their vulnerability as human beings, and instead sees only the prefabricated image. And this image, this narrative, supplies 'reasons' why an injury to Muslims (or Jews or feminists or intellectuals or Roma) is justifiable.

The depressing thing about looking at such forums is that it has all happened before. It's not new. The patterns of perception are not original; they have historical models. Always the same motifs, always the same images, always the same stereotypes are quoted and repeated here as if they had no history. As if no one remembered any more the context in which they originated and were misused once before. As if it was all new and original: the hatred of strangers, the elimination of everything different, the shouting in the streets, the slandering and terrorizing graffiti, the invention of a 'we' as a nation, a people, *das Volk* – and the construction of the others who allegedly do not belong to it as 'degenerate' and 'antisocial'.

Even the template in which 'foreign men' allegedly molest 'our women' or 'our girls' – it has all been used before as a theme of Nazi propaganda. Again and again, anti-Semitic texts and caricatures warned of Jews allegedly assaulting 'German women'.[23] The term *schwarzer Schmach*, 'black disgrace', was used to stigmatize Blacks as a sexual threat to 'white women' in conjunction with images that are still, or again, in circulation today, in an almost identical style. Today, once again, it is 'foreigners', Black people or refugees who are branded as a sexual danger.[24]

This is not an argument against reporting on crimes committed by migrants. Obviously, every form of sexual violence must be reported. It is almost absurd to have to say that. But slow reporting, accurate and informed reporting, is preferable to quick and sometimes sloppy reporting. And, obviously, reflecting on such acts brings with it the question what social, economic, ideological structures foster or facilitate them – just as the exposure of the abuse scandals in various Catholic institutions involved asking what factors facilitated or fostered sexual violence against children by Catholic clerics. In that case too, it was necessary – and possible – to offer a nuanced analysis that examined the religious dogma of celibacy, the stigma against homosexuality, the special constellation of power and trust between priests and children, the conspiracy of silence – in addition to the individual biographies of the perpetrators. This debate was possible without being driven by a hermeneutic of suspicion against Catholics per se, whether as individuals or as a community. No one demanded of random Catholics that they publicly distance themselves from the crimes.

The problem arises only when reporting on sexual violence is largely limited to cases where the act can be linked to a certain suspect profile, while other cases involving other perpetrators are rarely reported. In this way the concept of migrants or of Black people is automatically linked with that of sexual violence. Just imagine the reverse situation: if every report on a crime committed included the information that the perpetrator was *white*. Every day. If every robbery, every case of child abuse, every assault, was attributed to 'the *white* man from Rochester' or wherever. If reports mentioning a criminal with black skin were suddenly rarer. Obviously, I am not suggesting that one crime or another is less newsworthy or less reprehensible; I am proposing a matter-of-fact view in which crimes and perpetrator profiles can be set in quantifiable and appropriate proportions.

Again: of course there are migrants who commit such acts. Not only individually, but also in groups – as the horrible assaults in Cologne on New Year's Eve, 2015, demonstrate. And of course it is necessary and appropriate to report on them, without compromise. In the case of Cologne, that means analysing the suspect profiles and the events of that day in all their depth and with all their nuances, and identifying all the significant factors that can foster such acts. These may include excessive alcohol consumption no less than machismo and patriarchal mentalities. And of course the contexts and discourses in which contempt for women and their self-determination is fostered and cultivated must also be examined. It is precisely these discourses and these ideologically prefabricated, misogynistic patterns that need to be criticized. But in such real-life cases, unfortunately, racist and sexist fantasies overlap – and in our articles and photos we must also critically reflect on this overlapping of reality and phantasmagoria. This is not as difficult as it sounds.

The discourse in the immediate context of the Clausnitz video does without the term 'race'. Instead, commentators mention 'culture', 'immigrant background', 'religion'. These are code words used to camouflage the social taboos of racism and anti-Semitism without changing the underlying ideology. The group-focused hostility is still there; the comments still associate groups with ahistorical, immutable attributes. Only the term 'race' is missing. The same structure of exclusion is at work using the same images and themes – only with different words. The 'signal words' that would make it easier to recognize the political intention are missing. That is why it is now 'Western civilization', the 'people', the 'nation' that must be protected, without describing precisely what one or another of these things is supposed to be.[25]

There is no playful element in the world presented here; nor is there any element of chance. Every event, no matter how contingent, is given a meaning, and an intention is suspected behind it. There is no such thing as mere human weakness or accident. Every mistake is assumed to be intentional, every coincidence a conspiracy aimed at oppressing or harming the speaker's own group. The central theme of Facebook pages such as 'Döbeln Fights Back', and countless other publications of its kind, is the alleged 'replacement' of the population, the displacement, controlled by the authorities, of 'the people' by everything viewed as foreign: refugees, immigrants, non-Christian, non-white people. The scenario of civil war, both dreaded and yearned for, is the theme that runs through this conceptual world like a *basso continuo*.

The narrative that is constantly repeated in this context is an apocalyptic one: the old story of the downfall, the oppression, of one's own people, dramatically heightened to stylize one's own mission as especially existential, as destiny. The world is divided into the citizens of a shrinking or dying Nation on one side and those allegedly pursuing its demise on the other. The enemy camp includes all those protagonists of civil society who are naturally willing to help and show solidarity with the refugees: they are labelled 'do-gooders' or 'welcoming committees' (as if either were anything to be ashamed of).[26]

External criticism of the hatemongers' own practices and beliefs is not even deemed worthy of discussion. The fortified front, the polarized view of the world as 'self' and 'other', 'us' versus 'them', repels criticism to begin with, discrediting it as censorship, as repression, as manipulation of those who are fighting the one true and just struggle for their country, their people, their nation. This has established a closed world of ideas that considers itself immune to objections and doubts. Not those who intimidate women and children or set fire to refugee shelters are challenged, but those who criticize such acts. Critical reporting is merely evidence of an evil 'fake news' media which is unable to honour the heroically patriotic rebellion. In such a state of paranoia, everything only confirms the haters' own projection and even their own aggression can be idealized as self-defence.[27]

It is not easy to study such websites for long. As a homosexual and an intellectual, I belong to two of the social groups that are particularly hated in this context. I do not identify myself with a group, but that is irrelevant to the haters. In this template, people like me, with all their different references and inclinations, are not visible as individuals anyway. Although I have never turned out to welcome a coach full of arriving refugees, I am one of those the haters despise. For the way I love, and for the way I think and write. But at least it is for something I *do*. That in itself is almost a privilege. Others are hated and despised for the colour of their skin or for their bodies. I am white, and I have a German passport – both of these attributes are contingent. And both of them distinguish me from others who are more vulnerable to this hatred and this contempt than I am because they are Black or Muslim or both, or because they have no papers.

But this hatred affects not only those it seeks out as its objects. Web pages like 'Döbeln Fights Back' disturb me not only because they contain anti-intellectual or homophobic arguments. Inhumane argumentation disturbs me. Exclusionary arguments against a universal 'we' disturb me. It doesn't even matter *who* is construed as the invisible or monstrous Other. The hatred could be directed against left-handed people or Wagner fans. What disturbs me is the very mechanism of exclusion and the outrageous aggression with which people whip up hatred against people.

*

The Facebook page in question hosts a discourse about the video from Clausnitz among only a small circle of participants. Add to it all the other districts and towns where groups gather to protest against refugees and intimidate those who welcome them, and that would still be an isolated, marginal, extreme context. But surrounding this circle are the larger circles of all those who supply the ideological material, who produce the narrative models which then wander in the form of patterns and quotations through discourses online or in living rooms.[28] The *suppliers of hatred* include people who would never expose themselves as unrestrainedly as the agitators and the incendiaries in the street, preferring to give their 'concern' a civil façade. They are the people who dissociate themselves publicly from hatred and violence while constantly inciting them rhetorically. This strategy of intentional ambivalence is practised by AfD politicians, as well as by all the others who nonchalantly equate refugees with terror or crime, who do not recognize Islam as a religion, who mutter about defending the borders by force of arms.

And, not least, hatred and fear are fomented by those who hope to profit by them. Whether they reckon in the currency of ratings or of votes, whether they publish best-sellers with terrifying titles or clamour for attention with catchy headlines, the *profiteers of fear* may distance themselves from the 'mob' in the street, but they all know how to use it to their pecuniary advantage.

One organization which plays a special role among the suppliers of hatred and the profiteers of fear is the international terror network which calls itself 'Islamic State' and claims responsibility for a series of murders from Beirut to Brussels and from Tunis to Paris. The IS communications strategy pursues the same goal as the propagandists on the 'new right': to divide European societies by the logic of difference. With each new attack, IS increases the fear of Muslims – not incidentally, but intentionally. With each filmed massacre, each pop-cultural performance involving the execution of a defenceless hostage, IS consciously and deliberately drives a wedge into societies here – in the quite plausible hope that the fear of terror will lead to a general mistrust of European Muslims, ultimately isolating them.[29]

The segregation of Muslims out of a plural, open, secular Europe is the explicit goal of IS terror. The means to that end is systematic polarization.[30] All mixing, all cultural cooperation, all freedom of religion in the enlightened modern age is repulsive to the ideology of IS. The Islamist fundamentalists and the anti-Islam radicals thus form a curious pair of mirror images: they confirm each other in their hatred and their ideology of cultural or religious homogeneity. That is why reports about the horrible attacks by IS in European cities are a staple of right-wing forums. The objective violence, the real terror of IS, underpins the subjective projection of danger onto all those Muslims who are fleeing that same violence and that same terror. Every attack is used to claim justification for the cultivated fear of Muslims; every massacre is used to denounce the liberal, open society as an illusion. This also explains the reactions of some politicians and some journalists, who see in the terror attacks in Paris and Brussels mostly an objective confirmation of their own world view – and who seem to be more interested in being vindicated than in the grief of the victims' families.

The enablers and promoters of hatred include, furthermore, the people who do not intervene: those who, although they do not commit such acts themselves, sympathetically tolerate the acts of others. Hatred could never develop such force, could never break out and explode all over the country so persistently, so continuously, if it were not for the clandestine tolerance of people who, while perhaps not approving of violence and intimidation, nevertheless despise the object against which hatred erupts. Rather than doing their own hating, these people let others *hate for them*. Perhaps they are just apathetic, just lazy. They don't want to get involved or take on a commitment. They don't want to be bothered by these unsavoury disputes. They want to go on leading their peaceful day-to-day lives, undisturbed by the increasing diversity and complexity of a modern world.

These people include the prosecutors who hesitate to investigate attacks perpetrated against refugees or their shelters or against gays. They include the police officers who predominantly treat ethnic Germans as credible witnesses, and do not ask others what they saw or heard. They include all those who, although they

abhor Jews or Muslims or Roma, restrain themselves
from expressing their contempt, phrasing their rejection
cautiously – not as blind hatred, but as a careful
concern. They say that the people who attack refugee
shelters or press teams, who rant against 'elites' or
'Washington', have been left behind socially, that they
need to be taken seriously, that their feelings must not
be condescendingly ignored.

The hatred expressed in Clausnitz is not something
that exists only on the margins. This hatred has long
been prepared and tolerated, supplied with arguments
and approval, from the centre of the society. It doesn't
take much to do that. All it takes is the constant, quiet
devaluing or doubting of the rights of people who
already have fewer rights. All it takes is the constant,
repeated mistrust towards migrants in government
agencies; the especially eager or rigid screening of
Roma by individual police officers; the loud taunting of
trans persons in the street, or their quiet humiliation in
the law; the muttering about a 'gay lobby'; or the kind
of criticism of Israel that starts with 'It's not politically
correct to say this, but ...'. It is this massive amalga-
mation of practices and habits, of clichés and jokes, of
spiteful little remarks or gross insults that come out so
casually as to seem harmless, but that grind down all
the people who have to put up with them.

This is not hatred. Nor is it physical violence. And
hardly anyone who acts in this way sees himself or
herself in the same company as those people standing
in the road shouting out their contempt. But their quiet
tolerance or clandestine approval enlarges the space
of power in which people who deviate from the norm
cannot feel safe, included, accepted. This produces
zones that are unliveable, inaccessible, to many people.
Wherever people who believe differently or love differently are made invisible, wherever they are overlooked
as if they were not human beings of flesh and blood, as

if they had no shadow. Wherever people who do not match the norm are knocked to the ground, wherever no one helps them back up again, wherever no one apologizes; wherever those who deviate slightly from the norm are made into something monstrous – there are *accomplices to hatred.*

*

There is also a second video, by the way. It was shot later, by one of the refugees. The image format is the vertical screen of a smartphone between blurred left and right borders. The video shows what hatred does; it shows the effect hatred has on the people it is aimed at. On a floor indoors sits one of the refugees from the coach, a veiled woman, screaming and crying. She slaps her knees with both hands over and over again. A young woman crouches next to her, trying to calm her. But she will not be calmed. She can no longer suppress all the fear, all the despair – the fear she brought with her and the despair that has just burst forth. Her weeping is desperate, uncontrolled, abandoned.

The camera pans round, revealing a simple room, apparently in the shelter into which the refugees have finally been brought from the coach.[31] There they sit, on the floor or on chairs at a small table, mute, exhausted; they lean on the walls or on one another, evidently shocked that their long trek still has not taken them out of range of violence, that they still have not arrived in a place where they can rest, where they no longer have to be on the alert, where they can finally live free of fear. They do not say that in so many words in this video – only this one woman cries out her desperation.

We do not know what she and the other passengers from the coach have experienced in the countries they come from. We can only surmise what they have seen of war and expulsion in Lebanon, Iran, Afghanistan or

Syria. What they have fled from, whom they have had to leave behind, what scenes of horror replay in their minds at night – this video shows us none of that. But what a shameful experience they have been exposed to here is plain to anyone who has seen this video and is able to perceive something other than his or her own monstrous projection.

There is yet another story to be told about Clausnitz. A story of different people from those who claim to be 'the people'. They do not belong to that 'we' that unites in hatred and shouting – and hence they have garnered less attention. Nor has a big audience formed around them; they are not surrounded by any claque. Nonetheless, they too belong to Clausnitz. If you want to hear their story, you have to look for them, because they are quieter than the haters. One of these quieter people of Clausnitz is Daniela (who prefers to be mentioned only by her first name). She is almost amazed that someone is interested in her point of view. After an email exchange, she agrees to a longer telephone interview in which she describes how she experienced that evening in Clausnitz.

A day before, a few members of the local 'Asylum Network' had met to think about the best way to greet the new arrivals. They had asked themselves, Daniela relates, what they could say to welcome the refugees. As a small gesture they brought fruit baskets, along with their prepared greetings, to the shelter in Clausnitz. Together with the other activists, Daniela observed the events from the shelter the refugees were supposed to move into. They were safe there. Daniela and her colleagues had been verbally attacked before. She recounts that, on the same day, a woman from the network had received a threat that her house would be set on fire.

Daniela sees more and more people gathering in the road to protest. She does not join them, although they are people she knows. She keeps her distance. They are neighbours from Clausnitz. Men with families among them. Some of them have brought their children along, as if intimidating refugees was something children should experience first-hand as early as possible. Daniela stays in the building as a tractor appears and blocks the road some fifty yards from the shelter. 'We had a bad feeling. We didn't know what to do. But it was clear that something was brewing.' When the coach finally arrives, when the situation escalates, when more and more people crowd in front of the refugees shouting their hatred at them, Daniela sees no 'invaders', no 'specialists in theft and robbery', no 'foreigners' molesting 'our women'. She sees people being threatened. 'I could see the fear in their faces. I was so sorry for the refugees.'

The plan to house refugees in the town had been discussed as early as January at a meeting in the Clausnitz sports hall. Some of the people attending had expressed the fear that the foreign men could harass women and girls in the town. But what if, the objection was raised, it was women and children who were to be sheltered in Clausnitz? Yes, that would be different. Daniela remembered those words when the coach arrived full of women and children – and the difference no longer mattered. Hatred blotted out all inhibitions. There were no longer any differences, any fine distinctions, any individuals. The onlookers could not understand why, in this situation, the police didn't push back the blockaders, why they didn't order them to disperse.

Everything Daniela and the others had planned to say in welcome had become inadequate. 'The first woman I was finally able to help couldn't go on, she couldn't walk. She cried and screamed. She fainted. We had to carry her into her room.' Daniela stayed by the woman. For hours. She talked with her, although they had no common language. She didn't go home until shortly before midnight. She left the fruit basket there. What became of the haters in front of the coach? The moment the refugees were inside the shelter, Daniela relates, it was suddenly quiet. Very quiet.

*

Clausnitz is just *one* example of hatred and of the patterns of perception that prepare and shape it, that make people invisible and at the same time monstrous. In Clausnitz, the victims were a coachload of refugees. In other cities, in other regions, the victims are people with a different skin colour, a different sexuality, a different faith, an ambiguous body; the victims are young or old women, people wearing a kippah or a headscarf, people without a home or without a passport – whatever is made to fit as an object of hatred. They are intimidated, as in this case, or criminalized; they are pathologized or deported, attacked or insulted.

They are harmed, one way or another. But how badly they are harmed depends on whether other people stand by them. 'Rage is vented on those who are both conspicuous and unprotected', Horkheimer and Adorno wrote. That is a call for state institutions, for police and prosecutors, to take action against the people who occupy the public space with their hatred and their violence, transforming it into zones of fear. But it is also a call to everyone to be alert whenever someone is in danger of sinking in the mud of humiliation and contempt, whenever the flood of insults and hatred swells, whenever a gesture is all that is needed, an objection or a consolation, for the ground on which all of us can stand to become solid once more.

Hatred and Contempt, Part 2: Institutional Racism (Staten Island, New York)

> 'I wanted quite simply to be a man among men. I would have liked to enter our world young and sleek, a world we could build together.'
>
> Frantz Fanon, *Black Skin, White Masks*

What do they see? What do they see that I don't? The video, in the unedited version found on YouTube, runs eleven minutes and nine seconds.[32] The African American man Eric Garner stands on the pavement in broad daylight in front of a cosmetics shop. He is wearing a grey T-shirt, beige knee-length trousers and trainers. He is talking with two white policemen in plainclothes, Justin D. and Daniel P., who have taken up positions on either side of him, both with baseball caps pulled down low.[33] D. shows Garner his ID and says something unintelligible. Garner spreads both arms: 'Get away? For what?' No weapon, nowhere. He does not attack the officers. In fact, he hardly moves as he talks. He makes no move to run away. The gesture of outstretched arms is unmistakable. Eric Garner cannot understand why the officers are bothering him: 'I did nothing.' What D., the officer in the right half of the frame, says in reply is not clearly audible, but apparently it has to do with an accusation that Garner was selling 'loosies', untaxed single cigarettes. Eric Garner throws up his hands. 'Every time you see me, you want to mess with me. I'm tired of it.' He refuses to be searched because he does not understand why the officers should stop him and accuse him. 'This stops today. [...] Everyone standing here will tell you I didn't do nothing.'[34]

'Everyone standing here' refers to the onlookers. And in fact, uninvolved passers-by intervene. They do not just watch, as those in Clausnitz did; they act. Perhaps because they are *not* uninvolved. Perhaps because they know that the same thing could happen to any one of them. Every day. Just because their skin is not white. First there is the Puerto Rican neighbour who films the events with his phone, Ramsey Orta. His voice is heard repeatedly from behind the camera, commenting on what he is filming, speaking half to the camera, half to other passers-by. At the very beginning he can be heard confirming what Eric Garner says. 'He ain't do nothing.' One of the policemen then tries to chase the annoying witness away. But he identifies himself as a resident and stays where he is. He continues filming, whether the officer likes it or not. The policemen don't like being filmed, but it does not bother them enough to make them let Eric Garner go. Maybe they feel justified in their actions. Or maybe they just expect to be exonerated after the fact. There is another witness who intervenes. The video shows a Black woman who steps up with a notepad and asks the officers for their names. But even that does not hinder them in their subsequent actions.

For minutes, Eric Garner holds a discussion with the officer D. Garner explains that he has only broken up a fight. Nothing more. Again and again, he says he has done nothing. Again and again, the witness's voice off camera confirms Garner's version. After a while, the policeman in the background, Daniel P., can be seen talking into his walkie-talkie, apparently summoning reinforcements. Why? Eric Garner is quite tall and heavy, but he threatens no one. He poses no danger to anyone in this situation. And, most importantly, it is still unclear what he is supposed to have done wrong. Why the officers want to arrest him is not comprehensible. Perhaps because he has no ID? Because he refuses to be searched? What do the officers see? Why can't they leave this large, slightly awkward-looking man in peace? Although he has been known to sell 'loosies' in the past, there is no indication that he was intending to sell untaxed cigarettes on this afternoon in July 2014 in front of the Bay Salon in Tompkinsville, Staten Island. No bag, no rucksack in which he might have hidden the merchandise. What do they see?

There is no sign of anger in these recordings, no aggression. Nothing to indicate that the situation may escalate to violence. In Garner's tone there is more despair than anger. Nor do the two muscular officers look particularly alarmed. They must have been trained for exactly such situations. There are two of them; they can call in reinforcements at any time. The man in the shorts is not threatening them. After more than four minutes of conversation, Justin D. takes the handcuffs from his belt. He and Daniel P. advance towards Garner from the front and the back simultaneously. Eric Garner says, 'Please don't touch me', and twists his torso as P. tries to seize him from behind. He does not want to be arrested.[35] Perhaps his action is interpreted as resisting arrest. But Garner does not strike either officer. He does not attack them. He keeps both hands in the air – even while the officer behind him takes him in a choke hold. Two uniformed officers arrive, and all four pull and push Eric Garner to the ground, where he lands on his hands and knees. P. is still choking him from behind. He lies on top of Garner and continues to hold his neck in a choking grip. What do they see?

In his classic 1952 work of postcolonial theory, *Black Skin, White Masks*, the French psychiatrist, politician and writer Frantz Fanon describes the white perception of a Black body:

> The N. is an animal, the N. is bad, the N. is wicked, the N. is ugly; look, a N.; the N. is trembling, the N. is trembling because he's cold, the small boy is trembling because he's afraid of the N., the N. is trembling with

cold, the cold that chills the bones, the lovely little boy
is trembling because he thinks the N. is trembling with
rage, the little white boy runs to his mother's arms:
'*Maman*, the N.'s going to eat me.'[36]

When a Black body trembles, Fanon writes, a white
child who has been taught to be afraid of the Black
body cannot interpret the trembling as a symptom of
cold, only as a sign of anger. A white child, Fanon
writes, grows up with associations that connect a Black
body with an animal, with something unpredictable,
something wild, dangerous; he sees a Black body and
immediately thinks of the attributes 'bad', 'wicked',
'ugly'; he immediately thinks, 'He wants to eat me.'

Perception – the visible field – is not neutral, but
shaped by historical templates, so that only what fits the
template is noticed and perceived. In a society in which
the trembling of a Black body is still interpreted as an
expression of anger, in which white children (and adults)
are still trained to see Blacks as something to be avoided
or feared, Eric Garner (or Michael Brown or Sandra
Bland or Tamir Rice, or all the other victims of white
police violence) are *seen* as threatening even though
they present no danger. After generations of training in
such perception, a real fear is no longer necessary as a
reason to abuse the Black body. The fear has long since
been transformed and inscribed in the police's institutional self-concept. The racist template which perceives
something frightening in any Black body has been
translated into the attitude of white police officers who
regard it as their job to protect society from exactly this
imaginary danger. They do not need to feel acute hatred
or acute fear as individuals in order to curtail the rights
of Blacks. And thus the Black body is seen as a threat
even when it is helpless and half-dead.[37]

Garner lies on his side on the ground under a tangle
of police officers, his left arm bent behind his back,

his right arm outstretched on the pavement. The first policeman is still hanging onto his neck. All of them together turn the defenceless Garner on his stomach. What do they see? 'I can't breathe': four minutes and fifty-one seconds have passed in the video when Eric Garner says these words for the first time; 'I can't breathe' is heard a second time at 4:54, when five officers are visible in the frame, all abusing this Black body. They don't stop. Although they all must hear Garner's desperate cry. The officer who brought him down with the choke hold is now kneeling and pressing Garner's head onto the pavement with both hands. 'I can't breathe': 4:56; every two seconds it bursts out of him; 4:58, 'I can't breathe', 'I can't breathe', 'I can't breathe', 'I can't breathe': eleven times the asthmatic Eric Garner gasps that he cannot breathe. He is not heard again after that.

An officer takes up a position in front of the camera, screening off the scene. The voice off camera says, 'Once again, police beating up on people.' When the view is clear again, Eric Garner is lying on the ground with several policemen still crouching on and around his inert body. The cameraman is heard: 'All he did was break up a fight, and this is what happens.' A minute later, Eric Garner is still lying there. To say it plainly: a *human being* is lying on the ground. Unconscious. But no one thinks of taking the handcuffs off the helpless person. No one tries to resuscitate him. The officers surrounding him merely lift his lifeless body and set it down again. Like an object. They do not attend to the person; evidently they do not see him as a person. Nor do they look upset or desperate about what they have done. As if the condition to which they have reduced Eric Garner by their violence is the best condition in which a Black body can be.

'The ease of remaining ignorant of another person's pain', Elaine Scarry writes in 'The Difficulty of

Imagining Other Persons', 'even permits one to inflict it and amplify it in the body of the other person while remaining immune oneself.'[38]

The only thing that helps to make this video bearable is the witness's voice. He cannot change the horrible events, but he does not look away; he watches. He creates an alternative public sphere, a *different way of seeing*; he situates and interprets the events differently. His commentary adds a critical perspective to what is happening. He describes what *he* sees: a defenceless human being, attacked by the police for no reason. 'They didn't run and get the n... that was fightin'; they get the n... that broke it up.' The witness filming, Ramsey Orta, is urged again and again to leave the scene. Finally he changes his position and films squarely facing the beauty salon in front of which Eric Garner is lying. There is a brief interruption in the video; how much time has passed is unclear. The film timer shows eight minutes when an officer finally approaches the unconscious Eric Garner and takes his pulse. After two more minutes in which nothing helpful happens, in which no one attempts cardiopulmonary resuscitation or any other lifesaving technique, the policeman who pulled Eric Garner down with a choke hold suddenly walks into the frame. Daniel P. He seems to be walking up and down aimlessly. The witness filming addresses him: 'Don't lie, man ... I was here watching the whole shit.' The policeman then approaches him, waving him off, as if it makes no difference what he has seen – as if only the view of a white police officer counts. The officer says, 'Yeah, you know everything.' And in this 'you' is the disdain of the power that is sure that this 'you' will never be equal; in this 'you' is the certainty that it will make no difference what this witness has seen, because the word of a white police officer is always believed over that of a Puerto Rican private citizen.

There is also a second video, by the way. From a different perspective. It was evidently shot from inside the beauty salon through the open doorway. It begins much later than Ramsay Orta's. Eric Garner is already lying inert on the ground. Around him are the patrol officers who have been called to the scene, occasionally patting the heavy body, turning it, feeling the pulse in the neck. One of the policemen searches Eric Garner's trouser pocket – but no one tries to revive the unconscious man. The voice heard off camera here is that of a woman: 'NYPD, harassing people ... he didn't do anything at all ... now they want to try and get him an ambulance.' Minutes pass without anyone helping. It looks as if the handcuffs still haven't been taken off Eric Garner's wrists. One of the officers takes a phone out of Garner's trouser pocket and hands it to a colleague. After about four minutes, another leans over Garner and looks at him. She feels his pulse and speaks to him; nothing more. It takes several more minutes before an ambulance arrives. Eric Garner is lifted onto a stretcher – the camera pans a little to the side and finds the officer Daniel P. He notices that he is being filmed and waves to the camera.

Eric Garner died of heart failure on the way to the hospital. He was forty-three years old. He left a wife, six children and three grandchildren. The medical examiner later found the cause of death to be 'compression of neck (choke hold), compression of chest', and concluded that a homicide had occurred.[39]

'Scared! Scared! Now they were beginning to be scared of me', Frantz Fanon writes. 'I wanted to kill myself laughing, but laughter had become out of the question.'[40]

The choke hold that killed Eric Garner was not spontaneous. Even though it may appear so in this scene. The police choke hold has a long history. In Los Angeles alone, sixteen people were killed by choke holds between 1975 and 1983. In New York, twenty years before Eric Garner, Anthony Baez, a twenty-nine-year-old man from the Bronx, also with chronic asthma, died from a police officer's choke hold.[41] In that case, the occasion was not an alleged sale of cigarettes, but a game of catch with a football which – accidentally, as the police confirmed – hit a parked police car. The choke hold that killed Eric Garner has long been illegal: the New York Police Department prohibited it in 1993. Nevertheless, the grand jury charged with investigating the circumstances of Eric Garner's death and the behaviour of Police Officer Daniel P. decided, after two months of proceedings, not to issue an indictment.

'There is nothing uniquely evil in these destroyers or even in this moment. The destroyers are merely men enforcing the whims of our country, correctly interpreting its heritage and legacy', writes Ta-Nehisi Coates in *Between the World and Me*.[42] There doesn't even have to be any malice. There doesn't have to be any acute, burning hatred. All there has to be, Coates writes, is the certainty of a legacy in which Blacks can always be degraded, demeaned or abused with impunity. All there has to be is the inherited notion of fear which always associates the Black body with danger and therefore admits any violence against it as justified. In this historically rehearsed perception, all concrete evidence of the objective helplessness or innocence of Eric Garner or Sandra Bland or the congregation of the Emanuel AME Church in Charleston, South Carolina, is discarded. In this legacy, white paranoia appears a priori as legitimate.

Although the choke hold that killed Eric Garner was an individual act, since it was only Daniel P. who applied it in this situation, it takes its place in the history of white police violence against African Americans which has been decried most recently by the Black Lives Matter movement. The fear of white

violence is a part of the collective experience of African
Americans, part of the heritage of slavery.[43] That is the
dreadful paradox: that the racist fear of the Black body
is socially accepted and reproduced, while the well-
founded fear of white police violence on the part of the
Black people thus stigmatized remains in the blind spot
of that same racism.

> It is not necessary that you believe that the officer
> who choked Eric Garner set out that day to destroy
> a body. All you need to understand is that the officer
> carries with him the power of the American state and
> the weight of an American legacy, and they necessitate
> that, of the bodies destroyed every year, some wild and
> disproportionate number of them will be black.[44]

Calling attention to institutional discrimination or institutional racism does not mean accusing every single
police officer of misconduct or of having a racist attitude.
Naturally there are countless police officers who abhor
and reject any kind of discrimination or violence against
Blacks. Of course there are tremendously conscientious
officers who revolt against the historical burden of
racism. And there are regional agencies which strive for
good relations with local Black populations, trying to
build up trust and rein in the violence.[45] Unfortunately,
however, both statements are true: there are many
police officers of individual integrity, and there is a
racism embedded in the institution of the police and in
its self-concept which is quicker to see danger in Black
bodies than in white ones. In its way, the police reflects
the division of society which is part of the everyday
experience of Black people in the United States.

African Americans continue to grow up in the
constructed 'contradiction' of being both Black and
American. Blacks supposedly belong to American
society, and yet they are permanently excluded from it.

Statistics continue to document the social division of the United States and the discrimination against Blacks. Of the 2.3 million inmates in American prisons, according to the NAACP, one million are African Americans. African Americans are six times more likely to receive prison sentences than whites. According to a study by the Sentencing Project, the average sentence African Americans receive for drug offences (58.7 months) is almost as long as the average sentence white criminals receive for violent crimes (61.7 months). Between 1980 and 2013, more than 260,000 African Americans were killed in the United States. For comparison, 58,220 American soldiers died in the entire Vietnam War.

People who are white often cannot imagine such an experience of structural contempt. It is easy for white people to think: why would Blacks be stopped and searched if they haven't done anything wrong? It is easy for white people to wonder why Blacks would be arrested without cause, why they would be beaten if they haven't threatened violence, why they would be sentenced to longer prison terms if they are guilty of exactly the same crimes as whites. A person who has not experienced injustice as part of their day-to-day life may wonder why there would be injustice in the world.

A person who matches the norm can easily make the mistake of thinking there is no norm. A person who resembles the majority can easily make the mistake of thinking that matching the norm-setting majority makes no difference. A person who matches the norm often doesn't notice how they exclude or demean others. A person who matches the norm often cannot imagine the effect of their words or actions because they take their own inclusion for granted. But human rights are the rights of everyone – not just those who share a resemblance. So we must be alert to what kinds of deviation, what kinds of difference are treated as relevant for inclusion, or relevant for respect and recognition. We must listen when those who deviate from the norm tell how it feels in their day-to-day lives to be excluded and despised – and we must look at the world, and ourselves, from the perspective of that experience even though we may never have had that experience ourselves.

A person who is stopped by the police for no discernible reason may find it inconvenient the first time, but they put up with it without resentment. But for a person who is accosted over and over for no reason, a person who has to put up with being frisked time after time – for that person, random inconveniences become systematic insults. That includes not only experiences of institutional racism or police violence, but also minor and subliminal impositions. Barack Obama spoke about these day-to-day affronts at a press conference after the killing of the Black youth Trayvon Martin. Obama spoke about himself, and at the same time about the experience of all African Americans who are regularly and systematically watched like shoplifters in supermarkets, who are refused business loans for no discernible reason, who hear the sound of car doors suddenly being locked in the street – always and only because they are perceived as a danger, as a threat, as monstrous others.

Among these impertinences, easily overlooked by those who do not have to experience them every day, is that of being mistaken for someone else. Not for someone else who bears a resemblance to you. Just for someone who has the same skin colour, as if all Blacks looked the same. I know this from my own experience, although not in regard to Black people. As a lecturer in the US, I once had three Asian American students in a seminar. They bore hardly any resemblance to one another. When they all sat in front of me in class, they were easy to tell apart. But when just one of them came to my office hour in the first week, I didn't

know which of the three it was. I think I managed to
conceal my confusion, but I was ashamed. I hope it was
simply a matter of my lack of experience. A German-
Japanese friend of mine in Berlin later consoled me by
explaining that some Asians have the same problem
with faces like mine. Perhaps it is not reprehensible to
have trouble initially with names or faces we do not
meet often. But it is reprehensible not to reflect on that
and make an effort to get to know the names and faces
better – and to recognize the people they belong to as
individuals. Because for the people who get 'mistaken',
not just once, but over and over again, the experience
leaves a lasting impression, not just of ignorance, but of
contempt. As if they – as individuals – were negligible.[46]

Humiliations of this kind, experienced regularly, lead
with time to a kind of melancholy. Everyone who falls
somewhere between invisible and monstrous knows it.
Having to explain oneself again and again, in day-to-
day encounters in the street, in bars, in conversations
with acquaintances or strangers, every day or every
week, having to defend oneself against false accusations, against resentments and stigmas – that not only
saps one's energy, it is also unnerving. Constantly
being offended by terms and laws that are ideologically
charged, by gestures and beliefs: that is more than just
irritating; it is paralysing. Being exposed to hatred, over
and over again, often makes people fall silent. A person
who is designated as perverse or dangerous, as inferior
or sick, a person who is required to make excuses for
their skin colour or sexuality, for their religion or even
just for their headwear – such a person often loses the
footing from which they could speak freely and easily.[47]

On top of that, there is a moment of shame which
is often ignored: it is unpleasant to have to point out
yourself when and how words or gestures, practices
or beliefs offend and exclude you. At least, I find it
unpleasant. I secretly wish *everyone* would notice an

injustice even if they are not personally affected by it. That is a part of my moral expectation of others, or – perhaps it sounds gentler this way – part of my trust in my own society: to be able to assume that not just the victims of humiliation or contempt will defend themselves – that it is not just they who feel offended by such insults – but *everyone*. That is why it is strangely disappointing when you wait for someone else to intervene – and nothing happens.

That is why it is always a struggle – not only against fear, but also against shame – to speak up for yourself. Any protest, any objection, requires mentioning the degradation, mentioning that you are offended. Hannah Arendt once wrote, 'You can only defend yourself as the person you are attacked as.'[48] In her case, she was explaining that she responded as a Jew when she was attacked as a Jew. But that also means always asking yourself what you have been attacked as, and relating to the attack as the identity from which you are answering: as the person who is invisible and monstrous to others? As the person whose day-to-day life is constrained and burdened by gestures and language, by laws and habits? As a person who has run out of patience with these frames of perception, these attributions, this hatred?

What makes it especially painful is that the deep melancholy of being disdained is something that is hardly presentable. A person who articulates their injury, who ceases to suppress their grief at these unending, unvarying forms of exclusion, is often accused of being 'angry' (the description 'angry Black man' or 'angry Black woman' is a stylization, an interpretation, of the powerless person's despair as a supposedly groundless anger), of being 'humourless' (a standard attribution to feminists or lesbian women), of trying to 'take advantage' of their painful history (attributed to Jews). All of these pejorative labels serve mainly to silence the victims of structural contempt: to rob them of the opportunity to defend themselves by attaching to them from the outset an attribution that makes it harder for them to speak.

People who have never been humiliated, who have never had to defend themselves against social contempt, people who do not find themselves framed between invisible and monstrous, can hardly imagine how hard it is to appear *cheerful and grateful* in the moment of offence or injury to avoid drawing on themselves the attributes 'angry', 'humourless' or 'greedy'. The implicit requirement to please remain 'calm' while responding to systematic insults or degradation is all the more onerous because it implies there is no reason to feel insulted or indignant.

That is probably the reason why, for me, the most moving and the bitterest moment in the Eric Garner video is not when he utters the often-quoted sentence 'I can't breathe'. For me, the most powerful moment is when, before the officers attack him, Eric Garner says, 'This stops today.' The despair in his voice as he says those words. 'This stops today': this is the voice of a man who can no longer endure being stopped and searched and arrested over and over again, who is no longer willing to accept his role in an unjust drama, the role of a Black man, expected to put up patiently with constant humiliation and degradation. 'This stops today' also refers to the gaze that makes people invisible or monstrous, that 'overlooks' and knocks down people like the boy in the subway, and sees people like Eric Garner as a danger even when they are lying on the ground unconscious and handcuffed.

Maybe it moves me so because to me it illustrates the person I would like Eric Garner to be remembered as: not just as the motionless body lying on the ground under a tangle of police, not as the person gasping 'I can't breathe' before he dies, but as the person who says, 'I'm tired of it: this stops today', the person who objects, who wants to interrupt the story of endless stops and searches, the long history of Black fear of white police violence. His cry 'I can't breathe' expresses pain and agony, and that is probably why it became a motto of the campaigns in the United States. It is well suited as an indictment of the endemic police violence. The cry 'I can't breathe', which must have been audible to each of the officers, documents their indifference: whether a Black man gets any air or not, whether he might die – that apparently does not matter to them. Only a person who is immune from serious retribution can afford to be so indifferent.

'This stops today', on the other hand, refers not only to the abuse itself, but to the centuries-old hatred that has long since cooled and solidified into institutional practices of racist discrimination and exclusion. 'This stops today' refers to society's toleration, its lazy condoning of what allegedly cannot be changed just because it is old. With his 'this stops today', Eric Garner also asserts his subjective dignity as an individual who is no longer willing to have that dignity contested.

And it is that dignity that everyone ought to be defending. 'This stops today', this hatred, this violence, in Staten Island and in Clausnitz. 'This stops today', the populist elevation of emotions to political arguments, the rhetorical camouflage, the 'fear' and 'concern' that clothe naked racism. 'This stops today', this public discourse in which every feeling of confusion, every inner meanness, every delusion and conspiracy theory is considered unquestionable, authentic and valuable, and hence inaccessible to critical reflection, and to empathy. 'This stops today', these templates in which hatred is channelled, in which norms are defined which can then be deviated from only at the price of stigma and exclusion. 'This stops today', this inner disposition that leads to some people being 'overlooked' and knocked down, without anyone helping them up and apologizing.

2

Homogeneous – Natural – Pure

Home is where one starts from. As we grow older
The world becomes stranger, the pattern more
   complicated.

T. S. Eliot, Four Quartets

The biblical Book of Judges narrates the old and still timely story of the exclusion of an 'other':

> And the Gileadites took the passages of Jordan before the Ephraimites: and it was so, that when those Ephraimites which were escaped said, Let me go over; that the men of Gilead said unto him, Art thou an Ephraimite? If he said, Nay; then said they unto him, Say now Shibboleth: and he said Sibboleth: for he could not frame to pronounce it right. Then they took him, and slew him at the passages of Jordan: and there fell at that time of the Ephraimites forty and two thousand. (Judges 12, 5–6)

The single word *shibboleth* (Hebrew for 'ear of corn') is used to determine who may cross the threshold – who belongs and who does not. The *desire* to belong is not enough; it is not enough to give up one's origins and to profess allegiance to a new home. Such a declaration must be tested. The word *shibboleth*, which one group can pronounce correctly and the other cannot, this accidental skill or lack thereof, determines who is declared a friend and who is not. This one word is the watchword that divides 'us' from 'them', the 'natives' from the 'foreigners'.

For the Ephraimites, the Book of Judges tells us, the test was both crucial and impossible. Their safe passage across the River Jordan depended on a tiny detail: the *sh* sound in 'shibboleth'. When they pronounced the watchword, it sounded wrong. 'They marked themselves as unable to re-mark a mark thus coded.'[1] The criterion for belonging is thus something that is given to one group and not to the other. For the people of Ephraim, it is evidently nothing to which they could profess allegiance. Nothing they could acquire or practise. There is only *one* chance and an impossible task. Nothing in the old story offers a clue as to what else might characterize a Gileadite. No religious or cultural beliefs, no ritual customs or practices; nothing is mentioned that might define their life-world and community. And no reasons are given why the Ephraimites are supposed to be unsuitable, unable to integrate, or dangerous. The mark of difference that was chosen in the word 'shibboleth' is as arbitrary as it is insurmountable – the mark by which the people are segregated not only as others, but as enemies, to be degraded or injured.

The old story of the shibboleth is still timely today, for it tells of all the arbitrary ways in which societies can repulse and disparage individual persons or groups. It can be read as describing the mechanisms of anti-liberal or fanatical thinking: the invention of exclusive norms and codes which pretend to define the only correct form of religion, the only authorized membership of a culture, a nation, a social order, and which supply that social order with a legitimation to commit violence against everything that deviates from its norms. The codes may be different, and so may the consequences of exclusion, but the techniques of inclusion and exclusion are similar. Which norms, which dividing lines are condensed into a narrative to delimit 'us' from the 'others', whether they are used to restrict social acceptance or to curtail civil rights as well – these are variable. Sometimes the shibboleths 'only' stigmatize. Sometimes they go further, justifying or initiating violence.

Of course, there is nothing wrong a priori with identifying practices and beliefs that constitute a social or cultural community. Naturally, private groups and organizations set up their own rules for admission. And religious communities likewise define certain rituals and tenets that are meant to distinguish the particular nature of their religion. For some, these include observing fixed days of rest; for others, rules of dress; for some, ritual prayer is elementary, as is giving alms; some believe in the Trinity, others in reincarnation. Naturally, these practices and beliefs also define boundaries between those who belong, or want to belong, and those who do not. Thus Protestants can be and want to be distinct from Catholics; likewise the followers of Mahayana from those of Theravada. That is their right. All these definitions are internally more controversial, however, and over historical time (and different generations) they are more fragile, than many would want to concede. And, most importantly, these communities are potentially open to people who want to join them. They invent and pass down narratives which permit thresholds of entrance and transition. And their differences from other communities do not automatically imply an authorization of violence.[2]

What I am interested in here, however, are the narratives in which social, cultural, physical codes are invented that purport to characterize a democratic state, a nation, a social order, and at the same time declare individual persons or whole groups 'foreign' or *hostile*, and exclude them from a legal community. I am interested in the dynamics of the radicalization of world views or ideologies observable today, the recurring motifs and concepts with which social movements and political actors try to justify their increasingly fanatical positions (and, in some cases, their violence). I want to examine the strategies of constructing the 'true' nation, culture, community – and constructing the 'false' others who are subject to contempt or attack.

'Difference is corrupted into inequality, inequality into identity', writes Tzvetan Todorov in *The Conquest of America*; 'these are the two great figures of the relation to the other that delimit the other's inevitable space'.[3]

Todorov captures the anti-liberal impulse very accurately, describing how visible or religious or sexual or cultural differences between people do not remain simply that: *differences* between people or groups. From difference is derived instead *social or legal inequality*. Those who deviate, however slightly, from oneself or from a majority set up as a norm are suddenly perceived, not simply as 'different', but as 'wrong', and thus declared outside the protection of the law. Only the one absolute sameness of an identity is allowed to count – and everything else supposedly must be excluded and rejected.

What kinds of constellations are there today in which chance or innate differences are selected and set as the conditions for social recognition, or even for human and civil rights? What happens when social movements or political communities want to set criteria for equal treatment in a democratic state, criteria which only a *certain* segment of the society's population fulfil – only people with a certain body, a certain way of believing, or loving, or speaking? And what happens when these characteristics are supposed to determine who is accorded full civil rights or human rights, and who can be degraded and abused, expelled or killed?

To illustrate this using surreal examples: If only left-handed people were accorded freedom of opinion and free speech; if only persons with perfect pitch were accepted as apprentice cabinet-makers; if only women were admitted as witnesses in court; if the state schools observed only Jewish holidays; if only homosexual couples were allowed to adopt children; if people who stammer were denied admission to public swimming pools; if Manchester United fans were denied the right to assemble; if only people with a shoe size of eleven or greater could become police officers – then there would be arbitrary codes that determine each individual's social recognition, rights and freedoms, and access to opportunities and positions. It would be easy to see that the given criteria for inclusion or access are irrelevant to the abilities needed to exercise a certain office, to perform certain duties – or irrelevant altogether to the right to live a free, self-determined life.

Many common forms of discrimination and exclusion are no less arbitrary and absurd than the hypothetical examples listed above. But the narratives in which they are passed down (or the laws in which they are enshrined) are such long-standing traditions, the shibboleths they contain have been repeated so often, that, dubious as they are, they no longer attract attention. The norms which include and exclude need only to be very old in order to disappear in the blind spot of social perception. Other dividing lines that separate 'natives' from 'foreigners', 'true' families from 'false' ones, 'real' women from 'fake' ones, 'authentic Europeans' from 'inauthentic Europeans', 'true British' from 'false British' – in every case, a 'we' from an 'other' – are new or have only recently been demanded so vociferously in public.[4]

It is worthwhile to look at these present-day mechanisms of inclusion and exclusion: at the stories and the watchwords that are used to sort and evaluate people. Who may belong and who may not, who is included and who is excluded, who is considered powerful and who is considered powerless, who is accorded and who is denied human rights – this must be prepared and rationalized in an apparatus of verbal and non-verbal acts, in gestures and in laws, in administrative precepts or aesthetic postulates, in pictures and films. Such an apparatus evaluates certain persons as acceptable, belonging, precious, and others as inferior, foreign and hostile.

*

Certain political movements today are particularly fond of asserting that their own identity is *homogeneous, original* (or *natural*) or *pure*. Whether to endow a nation or a region with special authority, whether to provide a religious community with higher legitimacy or to claim exclusive rights for a people, at least one of the elements *homogeneous, original* or *pure* is sure to crop up in the self-description of the 'we' being invoked – whether it is the 'original' British people delimiting themselves from Eastern European migrants or German PEGIDA supporters defending the 'pure' Occident against Muslims. Often we find all three. They can be found in all kinds of movements and communities, and they indicate the illiberal potential of such identity politics. Secessionist movements, nationalist parties and pseudo-religious fundamentalists may differ drastically in their political positioning or their ambitions, and they may advocate different strategies of action (or violence), but they are all driven by a similar notion of a homogeneous, original or pure community.

Homogeneous

'Long before language cuts the world apart and classifies it, the human mind forges an ordering system of categories.'

Aleida Assmann, 'Ähnlichkeit als Performanz' ('Similarity as performance')

Of the national conservative or right-wing populist parties that have been successful in local or national elections in Europe, almost all appealed to wishful notions of a culturally or religiously *homogeneous* nation or a *homogeneous* people. They include the 'Freedom Party' in the Netherlands (2012: 10.1%), the *Front national* in France (2012: 13.6%), the FPÖ in Austria (2013: 20.5%), Fidesz in Hungary (2014: 44.9% and the government), UKIP in Great Britain (2015: 12.6%), the 'Sweden Democrats' in Sweden (2015: 12.9%), the 'True Finns' party in Finland (2015: 17.7% and participation in the coalition government), the 'Danish People's Party' in Denmark (2015: 21.2% and participation in the government), the 'Swiss People's Party' in Switzerland (2015: 29.4% and participation in the government), and PiS, the 'Law and Justice' party, in Poland (2015: 37.6% and the government).

To start with, the use of the term 'people' is ambiguous. What does it mean? Who is supposed to be 'the people'? Some political movements that invoke 'the people' do so not with anti-democratic or exclusionary intentions, but in an emancipatory and inclusive sense. They articulate statements such as 'We *too* are the people.' They feel excluded, wholly or partially, by political practices or laws which affect them while they are not sufficiently included in the decision-making processes. They feel insufficiently represented, not only politically, but in the media as well. Many social and political movements, whether they position themselves on the left or the right, criticize the lack of citizen participation in the parliamentary democracy of their state or in the European Union; they find fault with political decisions that are insufficiently dependent on public (and hence transparent) processes; they deplore an insufficient legitimization of the political construction of the EU. In making such criticisms, they appeal to the republican promise of popular sovereignty.

In the tradition of Jean Bodin and Jean-Jacques Rousseau, 'the people' is conceived as a community of free and equal individuals, endowed with a sovereignty which it cannot abdicate. In this conception of popular sovereignty, legislative power lies with the self-determined citizens directly, not with their representatives. The people imagined here is one which is actually present and able to negotiate and decide its own fate. To do so, it needs political processes which create the actual body politic in a founding act that is continuously self-renewing. In this republican tradition, the people is not necessarily something given, but something which develops through negotiation and which must be constituted in a social contract.[5]

*

Historically, however, this model too – the people of free and equal individuals – was a fiction. No republic has ever really accepted *all* people as free and equal. Or, to say it more plainly: never have all persons been accepted as human beings. Although the French revolutionaries did set the sovereign People in the space where the monarch had been, the plan of the democratic society was never as inclusive as it was claimed to be. Women and so-called 'foreigners' were excluded from the Rights of Man and the Citizen as a matter of course; an explicit justification was hardly thought necessary.

Ultimately, the democratic people, the nation which wanted to break with the privileges of the old estates, was able to constitute itself only in distinction from an 'other'.

This is evident not least in the language in which the idea of the sovereign people and the story of the social contract between free and equal citizens is narrated: from early on, the political order is described in *corporeal* terms. What was conceived as the democratic will of all (that is, all autonomous individuals) is suddenly transformed into the will of the whole – that is, of an undefined collective.[6] Out of a multitude of singular voices and perspectives, which must discover and negotiate common positions and beliefs in discussion with one another, arises the homogeneous unity of the whole. The metaphor of the society as a body suggests associations that are rich in political consequences: A body is solid and closed. A body is bounded and enclosed by a skin. A body is vulnerable to illnesses which are caused by germs and bacteria. A body must be kept healthy and immunized against epidemics. But most of all, a body is a unitary whole.

This biologization of political language (and hence of political imagination) encourages and connects with notions of hygiene, which are transferred from the context of medical care of the human body to that of a society: thus cultural or religious diversity is viewed as a danger to the national health of the people as a homogeneous body. Once our perception is guided by this biopolitical template, fears of infection by deviant, 'foreign' organisms become rampant. Any difference is then not simply different, but affects and contaminates the healthy, homogeneous body of the nation. The identity that this conceit engenders is a peculiarly hypochondriac one, always afraid of being infected by other practices and beliefs. As if every difference, any deviance from the national norm, however it may be defined, could become an epidemic through cultural or religious contagion. It does not say much for the strength of a 'cultural immune system' (to pursue the medical metaphor) if any encounter with other bodies is a dangerous threat and must be avoided. The biopolitical fantasy of 'the people' as a body that must be kept healthy encourages fears of even the slightest difference.

That explains why some people today are shaken in their self-concept even by a religious head covering, whether a kippah or a veil. As if the mere sight of a Muslim's hijab or a Jew's kippah could make members of the Christian faith break down and cease to exist as Christians. As if a headscarf could migrate from the head of the person wearing it to those looking at it. The idea would be funny if it were not so absurd. While one persistent argument against the headscarf asserts that it should be prohibited because the veil per se oppresses the woman (implying that no woman can ever want to wear one voluntarily), others see *themselves* and secular society itself as threatened by the headscarf[7] – as if the piece of cloth laid a weight not only upon the woman who wears it, but also upon people who look at it from a distance. Both objections fail to recognize that the presumed oppression cannot be exercised by a headscarf in itself, but only by persons or structures which impose a certain practice on women against their wishes. Consequently, both ordinances can be equally coercive: the commandment to wear a headscarf issuing from a patriarchal, religious milieu, and the commandment *not* to wear one emanating from a paternalistic, anti-religious milieu.

A secular society which instead guarantees the freedom to practise a religion and at the same time wants to protect and promote the rights of girls and women should always be guided by respect for women's self-determination. And that means recognizing that there may be women who *want* a devout lifestyle (whatever form that may take) or a certain practice. In the case of the headscarf, no one else has the right to declare the woman's wish irrational, undemocratic, absurd or impossible per se. Her wish merits the same respect as another person's wish to *oppose* such a conception of faith or such a practice, perhaps risking a conflict with their conservatively religious family. Individuals' subjective right to either of these decisions and life plans should be met with the same respect in Europe's liberal societies. The question of state employees wearing a headscarf is more complicated, since the fundamental rights of the individual (protected by Article 4, paragraphs 1 and 2 of the German constitution), including the freedom to exercise one's own faith, conscience, religion and world view, may come into conflict with the state's obligation to neutrality in matters of religion and ideology. Yet this issue is no different from the question of teachers wearing the Christian crucifix on a necklace in the classroom.[8]

But why should headwear make people nervous beyond all rational discussion? After all, these cultural or religious symbols indicate nothing more than that there are people who have a different faith. Is that the reason why they are so irritating? Because it is harder to deny diversity when it is visible in the public sphere? When the people who deviate from the specified norm of the nation stop existing only in concealment and in silence, but instead become visible and audible in everyday life: when they turn up in films, and not as a special topic – a problem – but perfectly naturally as main or minor characters; when they are described in school textbooks as *an* example of *a* way of believing or loving or looking; when different toilets are installed, making it clear that the earlier designs were not suitable as a generalized form (because using them was not equally pleasant for everyone) – then the imaginary body of the people is not threatened. All that happens is that the real and normal diversity of a modern society emerges from its invisibility in the shadow of the norm.

It is something else again when people try to idealize human rights violations as practices allegedly commanded by their religion. In conflicts of this kind, the state must uphold the rights of the individual against the claims of a religious group, or even against the individual's family: in regard to the horrible practice of clitoridectomy, or to child marriages, such intervention by the state – in the name of the constitution – is not only permissible, but necessary. A cultural custom cannot and must not subvert human rights.

*

The political and social players in Europe who are currently appealing once again to 'the people' and 'the nation' explicitly define the terms narrowly: they conceive 'the people' not as a *demos*, but usually as an *ethnos*, as members of a clan with (allegedly, at least) a common origin, language and culture. Those parties and movements which dream of a *homogeneous* people or a *homogeneous* nation want to rescind the idea of a legal community, whether national or supranational, of free and equal citizens. They want society to be bound together not along horizontal axes, but on vertical ones: ethnic and religious background, they say, ought to define who belongs to 'us' – and not common action, not common reference to a constitution, not the open processes of a deliberative democracy. The right to participation then becomes hereditary. And a person who did not inherit it because their parents or grandparents were immigrants is required to make special efforts, special declarations; to show a special adaptation to norms which are not applied, or not as strictly, to others.

An explanation why a homogeneous culture or nation is supposed to be *inherently* better for a modern state is rarely offered. And yet it would be interesting to know whether a religiously uniform society is economically more successful, whether a culturally uniform society is better able to cope with ecological crises, whether it produces less social injustice between its members, whether it proves to be politically more stable, or whether its members simply show more mutual respect for one another – such arguments in favour of homogeneity would be important. But the 'explanation' given for a homogeneous 'we' is often a simple tautology: a homogeneous nation is better because it is homogeneous.[9] Sometimes the argument is also advanced that the given majority is in danger of becoming a minority, and therefore excluding the others is just cultural or religious preventive care, so to speak. The slogans of the NPD (and lately the AfD) in Germany, UKIP in Britain and the *Front national* in France invoke this scenario: if it were more inclusive, the nation would not become dynamic and heterogeneous; it would be 'diminished', 'suppressed' or 'replaced' by people who are classified, on the basis of biologistic, racist concepts, as 'others'. But that still does not constitute an argument as to *why* homogeneity is supposed to be so important. It merely projects the proponents' own contempt for diversity and hybridity onto the alleged 'others'.

A much odder aspect of the current notion of a culturally or religiously homogeneous nation in a modern state is how ahistorical and counterfactual it is. The allegedly homogeneous embryo of a nation in which all the people are 'native', in which there are no newcomers, no different customs or traditions, no multilingualism and no different confessions – when is that supposed to have last existed in a nation-state? Where? This organic uniformity that is ascribed to 'the nation' is an extremely influential construction, but an imaginary one.[10] What people want and celebrate as a nation hardly ever corresponds to an actual community; it is always the manufactured image of a nation – and a society's subsequent approximation of this image. In other words, there is no original; all there is is the decision to invent and agree on a putative original which people are then expected to resemble.

As Benedict Anderson explained in his famous book *Imagined Communities*, all communities except archaic villages are ultimately 'imagined communities'. What the members of every modern nation in fact share is not so much common ethnic or cultural references (such as language, origin, religion), but rather the phantasm of communal belonging. 'It is imagined because even the members of the smallest nations will never know most of their fellow members, meet them, or even hear of them, yet in the mind of each lives the image of their communion.'[11]

The national conservative and nationalist parties, on the other hand, assert a national narrative that is *free of ambiguity*. Their national tradition must eliminate everything that tells of the disruptions, the ambivalence, the polyphony of the people's history. That is one of the reasons why the political forces with a nationalistic agenda in Europe are particularly interested in their countries' history departments, museums, cultural foundations, educational institutions and school textbooks: because they find uncomfortable all those voices and perspectives which contradict their construction of a homogeneous nation or a homogeneous people. Hence it is no wonder that the governing party in Poland, PiS, places great importance on celebrations such as the 'jubilee of the Christianization of Poland', or that Fidesz in Hungary tries not only to restrict the work of the independent media with new laws, but also to fill posts in cultural institutions with candidates whose artistic production does not challenge the neo-nationalist narrative. The AfD too, in its party programme, explicitly addresses cultural institutions as instruments of a highly charged concept of national identity.

But the homogeneity of the German people or the German nation, to which the AfD and PEGIDA are committed, does not exist. It can only be manufactured by excluding all the people they declare to be supposedly 'un-German' or 'non-Western'. Thus the parties work with various shibboleths to draw the lines that are supposed to divide 'authentic' Germans from 'inauthentic' Germans. Nothing is too trivial or too absurd if it serves this purpose. At a PEGIDA demonstration in Dresden, one participant paraded a staff through the street with a little pink toy piglet enthroned on top. Another wore a wool cap shaped like a pig's head. Is the pig the new mascot of the West? Is that what their cultural-ideological ambitions boil down to? Nothing against pigs, but if eating pork is really supposed to be a defining characteristic of Western identity, then maybe we should be worried about the Occident after all. Carrying toy piglets around at demonstrations is a rather harmless example, however: in recent months, severed pigs' heads have been dumped in front of mosques, and sites where mosques are planned, in many towns in Germany. The new fetish pork is not only a shibboleth with which to insult and intimidate Muslims, but also, of course, a traditional motif of anti-Semitism.

The brouhaha in May 2016 about the faces on the packaging of Kinder chocolates illustrates perhaps still more clearly what kind of an ethnically pure nation the PEGIDA supporters imagine: one which wants to see itself reflected only in racist terms as a community of white Christians.[12] In the run-up to the 2016 European football championship, the Ferrero company replaced the familiar blonde boy on its popular Kinder chocolate bars in Germany with childhood photos of the members of the German national team – including Ilkay Gündogan, Sami Khedira and Jerome Boateng. A PEGIDA organization in the state of Baden-Württemberg protested. They wanted Black Germans and Muslim Germans to remain invisible in advertising because they interfered with the constructed image of the homogeneous nation, the 'pure' German people.

The aversion to a heterogeneous society, to a people of free and equal citizens who share a constitution and a democratic practice, is articulated by other people as well besides the political representatives of PEGIDA and the AfD. The statement made and then forgotten by (or else just attributed to) the AfD vice-chairman, Alexander Gauland – that 'the people' appreciate Jerome Boateng as a football player but 'do not want him as a neighbour' (by which Gauland did not 'insult' Boateng, as some suggested, since his statement said nothing about him, but only about the supposed 'people' to whom Gauland ascribed a rejection of Black neighbours) – was an apt description of day-to-day racism in Germany, which has been documented and quantified in empirical studies.[13] In a representative survey (although a somewhat older one), 26 per cent of respondents agreed with the statement that 'people with a dark skin colour do not fit in Germany'. With that in mind, Alexander Gauland's statement could indeed have been intended as a critical analysis of racist attitudes. That cannot be determined from the quotation alone in isolation from all context. We may suspect, however, that Gauland was less concerned with challenging resentments and prejudices than with protecting them and legitimizing them as concerns to be taken seriously.

A few days later, Gauland commented in *Der Spiegel* on the pilgrimage to Mecca made by Mesut Özil, a member of the German national team and a practising Muslim. 'Since I don't follow football, it makes relatively little difference to me whither Mr Özil wanders. But in regard to civil servants, teachers, politicians and decision-makers, I would indeed ask the question: is someone who goes to Mecca appropriate in a German democracy?' Asked to elaborate, the vice-chairman of the AfD explained his position: 'I must be allowed to ask where this person's loyalties lie. Do they lie with the German constitution? Or do they lie with Islam, which is a political Islam? And does he intend to demonstrate, as he walks around the Kaaba, that he supports this political Islam? But I do not consider football players such as Mr Özil as decision-makers.'[14]

To begin with, it is surprising how often Alexander Gauland emphasizes that he is not interested in football. That is his right. But it is irrelevant to his line or lines of argument. If, as he insinuates, Islam and democracy are mutually incompatible, then a practising Muslim must be a problem, whether he is a football player or a judge of the Administrative Court of Appeals. Furthermore, in view of the celebrity of a member of the national team, Mr Gauland should be more concerned about the football player's influence than that of a civil servant. But never mind. The problem in Gauland's position lies in the fact that it casts doubt, not upon Mesut Özil's loyalty, but on Gauland's. He is the one whose statements are incompatible with the German constitution. All citizens have the freedom to practise their religion, and that includes pilgrimages to Santiago de Compostela as well as to Mecca. Even Alexander Gauland knows that. That is why he must also question whether Muslims are members of a religious community – he must deny that Islam is a religion. As 'evidence' for his thesis, Gauland quotes none other than Ayatollah Khomeini in stating that Islam itself is political. That is more or less like appealing to the Red Army Faction founder Andreas Baader for an authoritative definition of democracy. It is not Mesut Özil's loyalty to the constitution that is doubtful, but Alexander Gauland's.

Mesut Özil does not question that someone who holds the Christian faith, or no faith at all, is welcome in a secular democracy and deserves the same rights and the same protections of the state as everyone else. Mesut Özil merely practises his religion, without dismissing the different practices and beliefs of other people as disloyal or undemocratic.

Finally, this debate took a particularly capricious turn when Frauke Petry, then the spokeswoman of the AfD, first accused Özil of publicizing his pilgrimage to Mecca with a photo on Twitter (as if religion were something that must be lived in secret), and then accused him of not living 'according to the rules of Sharia' since the women accompanying him were not veiled. It remains unclear what her reproach against Özil really is: that he is a practising Muslim, or that he is not a practising Muslim. What is clear, in any case, is that the AfD claims to define not only what counts as a democracy (regardless of the definition given in the constitution), but also who counts as a Muslim. And, apparently, only an Islamist fundamentalist fulfils the AfD conception of a Muslim. An open, tolerant believer who, like most believers in other religions, observes some rules regularly, observes others only sometimes, and considers still others old-fashioned or impractical – to Frauke Petry, such a person cannot be a Muslim.

Original, Natural

'No one tells you it's because you are what you are.'
Cato, in Sasha Marianna Salzmann, *Meteorites*

The supposedly superior status of a 'we' is often embedded in a narrative that asserts a founding myth: 'our' belief or identity is better, more important, more valuable than others because it appeals to some kind of primal ideology or natural order. It is often a backward-looking narrative, presented as the tradition of the family or as 'our' way of life. In the past, when the society was purportedly still 'pure', when everyone supposedly shared the same values, the same dominant conventions – in this imagined 'before', everything was 'truer', 'more authentic', 'more real'. The present is often described in contrast as 'decadent', 'corrupt' or 'sick'. Individual persons, individual actions or positions are judged by the extent to which they 'authentically' conform to the purportedly original ideals.

The shibboleth being used here to devalue human beings does so by marking particular qualities, certain bodies or whole lifestyles as 'unnatural' or 'inauthentic'. The implication is that something – a person, a concept, a principle – is not as it used to be. Something has been changed. Something has not remained faithful to what it 'originally' was. Something is no longer the way nature designed or intended it to be. Something is challenging the natural, social order. Depending on the political or ideological context, the criticism of something 'unnatural' or 'no longer original' can be combined with an accusation of 'Westernization', 'apostasy from the true faith', the 'disease of modernism', 'sinfulness', or 'perversion'.[15]

The rhetoric of the 'natural' and 'original' usually turns up in reference to the same topics: the question what constitutes a 'real' man or a 'real' woman, and how to regard transgender or intersex persons; the question what can be considered a 'natural' sexuality, and how to respect gay or lesbian or bisexual or queer persons; and, not least, the question what counts as a 'real' family, and how to recognize all those families that exist outside of the traditional heterosexual father-mother-child configuration.[16]

For various reasons, the appeal to the 'naturalness' of gender has historically been both powerful and momentous. The notion of 'naturally' constituted genders has been transmitted through the Christian imagination, in which it is linked with the idea of a divine intention. This product of natural-divine creation is attributed a special validity, making it something sacrosanct. 'Natural', 'original' gender cannot and must not be thought of in any other way than that which the norm defines as 'normal'. By this logic, anything different, anything changeable, is seen as 'unnatural' or 'unhealthy', as 'not intended' by God, and hence can be disparaged as 'undesirable'.

One of the strategies for opposing this sanctified 'normality' of the sexes, refuting the claim that gender is naturally given, therefore consists in exposing that claim as an ideological position[17] and emphasizing instead the importance of social and symbolic factors in shaping gender. The argument that gender is socially constructed provides welcome political and normative freedom: for if gender, 'masculinity' or 'femininity', is not simply an innate physical fact, but the result of social and political conventions that define different modes of existence, then no fundamental 'normality' or validity can be inferred from it.

Nevertheless, I will leave aside the question whether a person's gender should be conceived as 'naturally' given or as a socially constructed. I will also disregard the question whether the heterosexual nuclear family is in fact historically older, more 'original', than other kinds of relationships or living arrangements, or whether that is a fiction. These are such important debates and such challenging questions that I could give no more than a fragmentary reconstruction of them here. At this point, I am interested in a different line of argument. I am interested in what significance the naturalness (or the originalness) of a body, of a desire, of a way of life is supposed to have for its *social or legal recognition*. In other words, what exactly do those people believe who believe in the categories of the 'natural' and the 'original'? If something first appeared in the world in a certain form, why should we, in the enlightened, post-metaphysical modern age, infer from that fact some legal right or some superior status? How is the legitimation of power linked to a certain idea of an original, natural order?[18] Why should something have greater or lesser value in a secular state, why should it be more or less entitled to recognition, just because it is supposed to have been this way or that 2,000 or even just twenty years ago? Does the constitution really accord a normative status to nature per se? In an era of cyborgs, 3D printers, biogenetic and synthetic innovations, reproductive medicine – in the Anthropocene epoch – what conception of naturalness is supposed to exist any more to which legal rights can be linked? Why should an altered or an ambiguous body be accorded less dignity, less beauty or less recognition?

*

A transgender person is someone whose spectrum of innate external sex characteristics, chromosomes and hormones is not in keeping with what they feel themselves to be. That would be one description. Another would be this: a transgender person is someone whose assigned gender does not match what they feel themselves to be. The first description refers to innate physical characteristics (or chromosomes and hormones). In the second description, the connection between the physical characteristics and the assigned gender is seen to be questionable or historically contingent.[19]

That may be difficult to imagine for people who feel all right and well settled in their assigned gender role. They often turn away or stop reading as soon as they hear the word 'trans' or see 'ze' and 'hir' as personal pronouns – as if people or phenomena which occur less frequently merited no attention or recognition. As if our supply of empathy was not sufficient, or not supposed to be sufficient, for everyone we encounter. And yet many people find it the most natural thing in the world to empathize with the rather improbable characters from Shakespeare's universe, or from Handel's operas, or from manga comics, and to try to understand their stories. After all, 'less frequent' does not mean strange or monstrous. Less frequent just means less frequent. The people we consider less common are probably just those about whom stories are more seldom told. And sometimes they are people with particular, rare qualities or experiences, whose longings and struggles for recognition reflect vulnerability as the very *condition humaine*. And thus it is precisely in the vulnerability of trans persons, in their search for visibility and recognition, that we find the mutual dependency that characterizes us all *as human beings*. In this way, the situation of transgender persons touches and affects everyone, not just those who live and feel as they do. The rights of trans persons are as important as all human rights, and establishing them and defending them is axiomatic to universalist thinking.

*

Many people are probably familiar with this situation, in a milder form, for many different reasons: not being able to identify with yourself in all qualities or characteristics; inwardly feeling something different from what is outwardly seen, believed or permitted; external expectations and attributions restricting your own freedom. In the case of transgender persons, this discrepancy between inner certainties and outer impressions or assigned roles concerns their gender identity. A person lives in a woman's body, yet sees himself as a man; or a person lives in a man's body, yet sees herself as a woman.[20] A person feels a longing, a need, a certainty that they want to (or must) live as a different person from the gender they have been assigned. A person has a given name from birth, yet they know that this name does not correspond to who they really are and who they want to live their life as.

I imagine this as a more extreme version of the irritation you feel when someone calls you by the wrong form of address or mispronounces your name: you wince. The wrong name or form of address can be physically irritating – no matter whether it is intentional or a careless slip.[21] Something in you squawks and wants to correct what was wrong. It begins with nicknames or endearments that you don't like or that don't fit you. You want to grin and deflect them – even if they are spoken with kind, loving intentions. More painful are insults, verbal attacks and slurs thrown at you in the street or on social media. Words that hurt reveal the special relationship between names and reality, knowledge and power.[22] A name is always a confirmation of a social existence. The way in which I am addressed defines my situation in the world. If I am constantly called by words that are charged or offensive, that shifts my social position.[23]

For trans persons, the birth name that refers to a gender role which doesn't fit them is thus a constant social disfigurement. They are supposed to answer to a name that rejects and denies their experience of life. Day in and day out, they are pinned to an unwanted gender assignment by the male or female given name entered in official documents. Worse still, and more humiliating, are their experiences at border crossings, when officers single out trans persons and interrogate them, or even physically examine them. And so it is vitally important for many trans persons to get their gender legally certified and change their given name or their gender in their birth registration, passport or driving licence.

*

Among the general public, Caitlyn Jenner has recently become the best-known image of a trans woman. After having had gender-affirming surgery, she portrayed an impression of the most 'perfect' femininity possible, in photos by Annie Leibovitz, on the cover of *Vanity Fair* magazine. Caitlyn Jenner, or the photos of Caitlyn Jenner, are associated with the idea that trans persons are always interested in a gender transformation – from man to woman or from woman to man – that is as aesthetically perfect as possible. In this interpretation, a trans person does not challenge the socially dominant gender images, but rather confirms the existing codes of masculinity and femininity. Even leaving aside her financial resources, her personal renown, and the concomitant media attention, the case of Caitlyn Jenner is by no means representative. This is not intended to diminish the respect she deserves for her courage. But for many trans persons, public visibility and acceptance are much more difficult to achieve because of their class, their skin colour, or their social marginalization. Although Caitlyn Jenner presented a particularly spectacular example of a trans woman, the lived reality of most trans persons is by no means as glamorous. In the United States, the unemployment rate among trans persons was 14 per cent in 2013, twice as high as the national average; 15 per cent had an annual income of less than $10,000, lower than all but 4 per cent of the overall population.[24]

Most importantly, though, there is not just one way of living as a trans person. There is an enormous diversity of trans persons, of experiences and performative practices of presentation and expression. Some trans persons quote the shibboleths that are currently accepted as prototypically masculine or feminine; others play on them and subvert them. The codes for masculine or feminine may be recycled or satirized; they can be confirmed or ignored, in speech or song, in drag or in vogueing, in dancing or dressing, with packers or binders,[25] with cosmetics or beards or wigs or shaves – or with nothing at all. Some people make every conceivable effort to pronounce or to imitate that *sh* in 'shibboleth'; others transform the whole password by processes of re-iteration, and with it the mechanics of exclusion and inclusion.

Individuals can differ widely in their desire to adjust their official gender to match their inner conviction and their experienced gender. Some people reject all gender categories because they find none fits them, or because they find such categories fundamentally suspect. Some people want to be recognized legally and socially in the gender in which they live – without having to have medical treatment. Some want to have all the primary and secondary sex characteristics that correspond to the gender they identify themselves as. For those who want to change or adapt their sexual identity, there are various paths of transition, which can involve hormone supplements or surgery – this too varies widely. *Trans* can mean 'from male to female' or 'from female to male', but it can also mean 'between male and female' or 'neither male nor female'. And it can mean that the binary categories 'male' and 'female' are inappropriate, or simply too limited. Some people, not wanting to be constrained in an 'either/or' gender role or in an 'either/or' body as defined by these categories, live in an 'elsewhere'.[26]

In fact, trans persons themselves disagree on the normative or political meanings of the different forms of transition – on what concepts of corporeality or 'naturalness' they affirm or challenge by their practices

and decisions: is a gender-alignment operation a kind
of 'mutilation' of a 'natural' body? Or is it only a
correction, bringing something into its appropriate form?
Or are bodies now, have they always been, products of
biochemical, medical and technological intervention, so
that any notion of an original, untouched body is absurd?
Is it a form of subjective freedom to want to shape,
cultivate, change yourself? Is it an emancipatory version
of taking care of yourself? Or is hormone therapy a politically suspect alliance with a pharmaceutical industry that
makes a profit from the fact that states want to regulate
and discipline people's pleasure and people's bodies?

To what extent do people who suffer under ascribed
gender norms, or who challenge them, ultimately
confirm those same norms? The trans man Paul B.
Preciado writes about these open political questions
among his own friends: 'I know they're going to judge
me for having taken testosterone [...] because I'm going
to become a man among men, because I was doing well
as a girl.'[27] That is indeed what some trans persons
want: to become a man like other men, or a woman
like other women. And what others want is to escape
these models, these standards of what is acceptable as
masculine or feminine. And there is also the important
question what a hormone treatment actually *does*. Does
a person who takes hormones automatically start assimilating to the dominant gender-role images? What does
taking hormones do to a person? Does the treatment
only change the person, or does it influence how others
think about the person? One answer to this question is
a medical one: when the testosterone level in the blood
increases in a body which is accustomed to a metabolism
based on the production of oestrogen, a kind of 'repro-
gramming' takes place: 'The slightest hormonal change
affects all the functions of the body: the desire to eat
and to fuck, circulation and the absorption of minerals,
the biological rhythms regulating sleep, the capacity for

physical exertion, muscular tone, metabolism, the sense of smell and taste – in fact, the entire biochemical physiology of the organism.'[28] But is the result automatically 'masculine'? Or is 'masculinity' merely the convention that a certain constellation of chromosomal and genital characteristics, and of gestures, practices and habits, is understood as 'masculine'?

*

For those who choose to make a transition, the path is strewn with incalculable internal and external thresholds.[29] The internal thresholds include not knowing how your own skin will feel, how your own voice will sound, how your own sweat will smell, how your outward appearance and your desire may change. 'I'm waiting for the effects of T., without knowing exactly what they'll be or how or when they'll become apparent', Paul B. Preciado writes about his decision to take testosterone for the first time.[30] Choosing to make a transition necessarily means letting yourself in for something dynamic and unpredictable – yourself, among other things. And, even if the transition involves nothing illegal, even if it takes place under a doctor's supervision and the state's administrative regulation, it is a path full of taboos and fragility. 'When I decide to take my first dose of testosterone, I don't talk about it to anyone', Preciado writes. 'As if it were a hard drug, I wait until I'm alone in my home to try it. I wait for nightfall. I take a packet out of the glass box, which I close immediately, to be sure that today, for my first time, I'll take one, and only one, dose. I've barely started, yet I'm already behaving as if I were an addict of an illegal substance. I hide, keep an eye on myself, censure myself, exercise restraint.'[31]

Another of the inner thresholds is the fear of losing social acceptance. Worrying about other people's constantly repeated questions, and the constantly repeated explanations that will probably be necessary to help acquaintances and colleagues understand the change. On the one hand, it seems obvious that the people in one's social environment would like to understand the process, and that they have questions which are well-intentioned. Addressing a person by a new name, a person you have always known by a different name, takes getting used to, of course. It probably takes some time before the new name feels as natural and familiar as the old one. There will be occasional mistakes, by accident and by force of habit. That is understandable. And that is certainly another reason why it helps to ask questions in order to understand the process better. On the other hand, though, it can be tedious for trans persons to be always expected to discuss their own transition. Sometimes they would like to be perceived as an individual over and above that aspect of their lives – as someone who plays drums or is raising a child or works as a lawyer. Another of the inner thresholds is certainly the fear of pain in connection with surgery. A transition is not a single act, a single surgical 'correction', but often a long sequence of operations, some of them painful and complex.

*

The external thresholds that precede a transition mainly include bureaucratic, financial, psychiatric and legal hurdles that are placed in the way of a sex reassignment. In Germany, the official recognition of trans persons with the gender in which they identify themselves has been regulated since 1981 by the 'Transsexuals Act' (*Transsexuellengesetz*, TSG).[32] The Act – titled in full the 'Law on Changing Given Names and Determining Gender in Special Cases' – defines the conditions which must be met before the state will fulfil a person's request

to match their given name to their subjective gender
(called the 'lesser solution'), or to change the sex recorded
in the registration of their birth, that is, to change their
officially assigned gender (the 'greater solution'). After
numerous amendments, the law no longer requires sex
reassignment surgery as a condition of changing the sex
recorded in a person's registration of birth. Rather, the
law provides for a change in the official record when
the applicant 'no longer *feels themselves as belonging*
to the sex indicated in their registration of birth' (my
emphasis).[33] What matters is thus not some kind of
naturalness or definitiveness of the body, or whether the
body corresponds in all characteristics to the person's
subjective gender. What matters is whether or not the
person *identifies* with their assigned gender. In a series
of decisions, the German Constitutional Court has come
around to the view that the person's psychological or
emotional identification alone should be assessed – and
not their physical characteristics. Thus the court's First
Senate argued in a decision of 11 January 2011: 'Since
the Transsexuals Act has been in force, new knowledge
about transsexuality has been gained [...]. Transsexuals
live in the irreversible and permanent consciousness of
belonging to the sex to which they were not assigned at
birth on the basis of their external physical sex characteristics. Their sexual orientation in their subjective sex,
like that of non-transsexuals, can be heterosexual or
homosexual.'[34]

Nonetheless, the free development of one's personality, guaranteed as a fundamental right by the German
constitution, has not been quite so free up to now
for trans persons. Their right to self-determination is
curiously restricted. People can decide for themselves
what they do with their bodies in infinitely many ways.
It is legal to use synthetic drugs or to emulate your
own aesthetic fantasy in your appearance by means
of plastic surgery; you are permitted to use innovative

medical and prosthetic technology to add to your body
or to substitute individual parts. People are allowed
to use in-vitro fertilization to initiate a pregnancy;
they can treat severe wounds and injuries thanks to
reconstructive surgery – all this has long since become
medical and aesthetic routine. But trans persons' free
development of their personality is still overlaid with
administrative requirements and overburdened with
biopolitical regulation and discipline. In view of the
many disciplines whose involvement is legally required
– therapists, expert witnesses and physicians – the
sociologist Stefan Hirschauer calls sex change 'a professional accomplishment'.

Thus the law demands an investigation of the matter of
'transsexualism'. The local court is instructed to obtain
two independent expert assessments from qualified
psychiatrists and psychologists stating that the trans
person's gender identity will not change. Without these
reports, the court may not change the official registry.
In these psychological reports, the experts diagnosing
'transsexualism' do not necessarily limit themselves to
judging (as the legislation stipulates) whether a person
feels themselves to belong to the other sex. They also
evaluate transsexuality as a disease and a 'disorder'.[35]
Such expert diagnoses are based on the classification of
'transsexualism' as defined in the ICD-10 manual (the
*International Statistical Classification of Diseases and
Related Health, 10th Revision*) issued by the World
Health Organization (WHO). Chapter V, Sections F00
to F99 of the ICD list psychological and behavioural
disorders, including Sections F60 to F69, 'Disorders of
Adult Personality and Behaviour'. Why? Why should
a trans person be classified as having a behavioural
disorder? The German Constitutional Court does not call
for such a pathologization. The court's only condition
is that a person feels they belong to the other sex – and
that that feeling can be expected to be permanent. That

is not a reason to define the person as 'sick', or their feeling as 'unnatural'. Many trans persons complain that a person who wants to change their name or the sex assigned in their birth certificate not only has to provide two psychiatric reports to the local court, but also has to supply the experts who write them with a credible narrative of their affliction. For some trans persons, who have experienced their previous life as one of terrible suffering, this is no obstacle. Some describe this suffering as living 'in the wrong body'. Others, however, describe their affliction as suffering from the perception and interpretation of their body as socially unacceptable. Some trans persons do not altogether reject the classification of their suffering as an illness, because they did in fact experience their lives before their rebirth in a different body and with a different name as terribly painful. For many other trans persons, though, the legally required psychiatric reports are an intolerable pathologization of their identity. Understandably, they object to being stigmatized as ill, as having a 'disorder', and they object to having to support that stigmatization de facto by cooperating with the process of psychiatric evaluation if they want to get the report they need.

In his book *The Elusive Embrace*, the critic Daniel Mendelsohn tells how he was marked by his study of classical languages. In ancient Greek, there is a typical sentence structure consisting of clauses linked by the words *men* and *de*, which can be translated as 'on the one hand ... but on the other hand'. The Greeks *men* pushed on; the Trojans *de* resisted. Thus these particles are used to form sentences that express an opposition. Mendelsohn describes how this structure of on-the-one-hand, on-the-other-hand gradually influenced his thinking: 'If you spend a long enough time reading Greek literature, that rhythm begins to structure your thinking about other things, too. The world *men* you were born into; the world *de* you choose to inhabit.'[36]

Thinking about masculinity or femininity is usually bounded by this structure of opposites, of either/or. Regardless of what is conceived to be masculine or feminine in a given historical context or a given culture, it is important that the supposedly 'natural' and 'original' outlines and boundaries of these categories are not blurred: that the essential differences are always discernible and validate the social order. The assertion that gender is naturally given always goes hand in hand with the claim that genders are immutably *unequivocal*.[37]

If gender is not unequivocal – if a person's body or lived gender role challenges the gender assigned to them at birth, or if a person challenges the whole binary gender categorization – then, even today, that person is ascribed a medical condition, a psychiatric disorder. What is declared to be 'original' or 'natural' in this context is no longer just a person's body, but the binary thinking itself, the structure of *men* and *de*. Persons who do not conform to this order are evaluated by experts as 'sick'.[38]

The issue of pathologizing trans persons involves not only the legal and normative consequences of such thinking in connection with the desire for recognition and changes to names and birth records. More importantly, the stigmatization of a 'disorder' strips trans persons of the political and social protection which they need – and which is their right just as much as it is that of every other human being. The definition of transsexuals as persons who not only deviate from a norm, but also have an alleged 'disorder', segregates and isolates them. All too often, unfortunately, this social defamation kindles contempt and violence, to which trans persons are particularly exposed in their day-to-day lives.[39] Trans-phobic persons and groups welcome the idea of a supposed 'illness' as a 'justification' for derision and hatred, for brutal attacks or sexual violence.

As the horrible attack in Orlando in June 2016 painfully demonstrated yet again, it is the experience of defencelessness that unites people who are lesbian, gay, bisexual, transgender, intersexual or queer.[40] However different we may be in other respects, however unique we may be as individuals, the feeling of vulnerability is something we all have in common. Always having to expect insults and assaults in public, never being certain what we are risking when we who love or desire or look *a little* differently than the norm-setting majority walk hand in hand or kiss in the street. Always having to reckon with abuse, always being aware that we are still an object of exclusion and violence for the haters. 'Gay spaces are haunted by the history of this violence,' writes Didier Eribon in his superb memoir *Returning to Reims*; 'every path, every park bench, every nook that is sheltered from prying eyes carries somewhere within it all of this past.'[41]

On 17 May 2016, the 'International Day Against Homophobia, Transphobia and Biphobia', the Trans Murder Monitoring Project published the following statistics: in the preceding four months of 2016 alone, 100 trans and gender-diverse persons had been murdered. From the beginning of monitoring in January 2008 to 30 April 2016, 2,115 people in sixty-five countries died of homophobic, trans phobic and bi-phobic violence. No less than 1,654 of those murders were registered in Central and South America. In the Hate Crime Statistics of the Organization for Security and Cooperation in Europe for the year 2014, the rubric 'Hate Crimes against LGBT Persons' lists 129 cases that were reported by police – significantly fewer than the reported number of hate crimes motivated by anti-Semitism (413) or racism (2,039). The OSCE statistics also list those cases which were not reported to police, but collected and registered by civil-society activists and organizations: forty-seven violent attacks with a racist background and 118 violent attacks against LGBT persons were registered in the same year.[42]

The hatred and abuse that trans and intersex persons experience is especially virulent. They are exposed to much stronger discrimination and more brutal violence than gay and lesbian persons. Not least because there are far fewer public spaces that are open to them and offer them protection.[43] In swimming pools, changing rooms and public toilets, they are constantly at risk of exclusion or harm. The special aggression that trans and intersex persons face is often kindled by the fact that trans-phobic persons and groups simply cannot stand *ambiguity* or ambivalence.[44] But whether something is perceived as 'ambiguous' or 'ambivalent' at all depends on the limited categories that are available. Contempt for trans persons is often cloaked in the assertion that one's own masculinity, one's own femininity could be endangered or devalued by the ambiguity of the gender roles that trans persons live. This is odd inasmuch as trans persons do not ask anyone else to change their gender identity – they only question the conditions under which their right to the free development of their personality is curtailed.

*

The topic of trans persons' access to public toilets has been hotly debated recently in the US. Eleven states sued Barack Obama's federal government because it had instructed the country's schools to let trans persons choose which toilets correspond to their subjective gender identity – regardless of the gender assigned them in their birth certificates. Some states protested with a lawsuit in which they accused the government of turning 'workplaces and educational settings across the country into laboratories for a massive social experiment'.[45] If protecting minorities, in law and in public buildings, from discrimination and violence is a 'massive social experiment', then the accusation is true.

It is indeed amazing how bitterly and excitedly people agitate against providing toilets to persons whose 'original' gender no longer corresponds to the one in which they live their lives. And at the same time, people who advocate opening toilets to trans persons, or changing the signs on public toilets, are often accused of having a fixation on the ridiculous idea that their emancipation should depend on something so banal. But – leaving aside the surprising underestimation of the importance of toilets which that accusation betrays – if the issue were really as ridiculous as all that, surely it could be resolved with equanimity and generosity.

What is so complicated about it? An open, just society is characterized by its ability to learn: that means not only that it allocates resources to developing solutions to ecological or economic problems, but also that it self-critically questions the criteria by which it grants social participation or political franchise. A learning society is characterized by the fact that it checks whether everyone really has all the same opportunities and the same protections, or whether there are visible or invisible barriers in the form of taboos or ideological shibboleths. This entails observing the effects of laws and their enforcement, and examining postulates that exist in the concrete forms of architecture or media. It should be possible to question these with a certain self-critical, ironic curiosity.

Of course there are news programmes in sign language and subtitled TV channels for the hearing-impaired; there are ramps and lifts to make train stations and public buildings accessible to less mobile walkers and wheelchair users; many restaurants display a tremendous willingness to make people feel welcome and cater for even the rarest food intolerances – and yet trans persons cannot be allowed to use the toilets that are appropriate for them? It goes without saying in our society that we make concessions to all kinds of cultural, medical and religious needs. It doesn't take much thought or energy – and financial investments are required only when material, architectural changes are involved. Guaranteeing safe spaces for trans persons should be equally uncontroversial – in swimming pools and schools, and in prisons, refugee shelters and immigration detention centres. In March 2016, Human Rights Watch published a report titled 'Do You See How Much I'm Suffering Here' on abuses against trans women refugees in American prisons and detention centres.[46] The report documents how transgender women refugees are held, not in women's prisons, but – on the basis of the 'original' gender assigned them at birth – in men's institutions. There they not only have to suffer body searches by male staff; they are also the victims of regular violent assaults. Because even the prison staff notice how brutally trans women refugees are mistreated and tormented in this environment, they often put them in isolation cells – 'for their own protection'. This expression redefines solitary confinement – ordinarily a cruel measure used to punish people who are already prisoners – as an allegedly considerate, protective treatment of trans persons.

*

And all this regulation and discipline has to be undertaken by state and society simply because gender and the body must be absolutely subjected to criteria of 'naturalness' and 'originality'? All the individual and collective suffering, all the exclusion, all the pathologizing are supposed to be socially acceptable just because an allegedly original order must not be questioned? What authority is being attributed here to nature in declaring it suddenly static and unquestionable – only when the purpose is to mark trans persons as 'others'?

Article 2 of the German constitution says every person shall have *the right to free development of their personality*, and it says the *right to life and physical integrity* and the *freedom of the person* shall be inviolable. It does not say 'semi-free development of their personality'; nor does it say 'those persons whose personality adheres to the gender assigned them at birth shall have the right'. It does not say 'the freedom of only those persons who conform to traditional notions of "natural" masculinity and femininity'. It says, 'every person shall have the right to free development of their personality'. Nowhere is it written that a person may not change or develop. On the contrary, the constitution protects the individual's freedom to act – as long as other people's freedoms are not violated. The constitution belongs to everyone, not just to the majority. And it is obliged to protect everyone – including those who deviate, in whatever way, from a majority.

It is not up to transgender persons to justify why they want to be recognized just as other people are. It is not trans persons who must explain that they are entitled to the same subjective rights, the same protection of the law, the same public access as other people. It is not trans persons who must justify the way they want to live. It is not trans persons who must explain why they are entitled to the right of free development of their personality: the burden of explanation is on the people who want to deny them that right. It is time to reform the 'Transsexuals Law' so that it upholds trans persons' right to self-determination with or without an expert's examination and report. A reasonable solution would be a simple application procedure like the one used in Argentina and Portugal: it should be possible to lodge a request for a change of gender with a register office.

The change in the civil register could then be confirmed by a simple certificate.[47]

'What is interesting about the peculiarity of Greek, though, is that the *men* ... *de* sequence is not always necessarily oppositional. Sometimes – often – it can merely link two notions or quantities or names, connecting rather than separating, multiplying rather than dividing.'[48]

It would be nice if this relaxed understanding of the situation were to spread: a structure that seemed to be polar can be replaced by a form in which different kinds of connections and associations occur. No one loses anything, nothing is being taken away from anyone, no one has to change when a society accords trans persons the right to free development. No person and no family is prevented from conforming to their own conception of masculinity or femininity. All that would change is that trans persons, as healthy, vital, free human beings, would be accorded the same subjective rights and the same protection of the state as all other people. That would not curtail or neglect anyone's rights. It would expand the space in which everyone can live together as free and equal citizens. That is the least we can do. We must not leave it up to trans persons themselves to sue for their right to the free development of their personality. We cannot leave those who are excluded or ignored to struggle alone for their freedom and their rights. It must be in the interest of everyone that everyone enjoys the same freedom and the same rights.

Pure

'Their minds are full: with lust for extermination and
the certainty of acting with impunity.'
Klaus Theweleit, *Das Lachen der Täter*
('The laughter of the perpetrators')

Another strategy for describing one's own group or
ideology as superior, for distinguishing an 'us' from the
'others', is through narratives that assert one's 'purity'.
The shibboleth used here to declare some people as
belonging and others as hostile is a division between
the supposedly 'immaculate' and the supposedly 'dirty'.
Persons who are deemed unclean or impure must be
singled out and punished. The propaganda spread by
Salafist jihadism, the ideological programme of the terror
network called 'Islamic State' (IS), is such a propaganda of
purity, intended to ennoble that organization's violence.

One might object at this point: Why study the
doctrine of a terrorist group? Is it not enough to know
that they kill people, deliberately and arbitrarily, in
Beirut and Tunis, in Paris and Brussels, in Istanbul and
Raqqa? Is it not enough to recall the despicable murders
of children in Toulouse, killed just because they were
Jewish? Or the murders of people in a kosher super-
market in Paris? Or the murders in the Jewish Museum
in Brussels? All merely because the victims were Jewish?
Is it not enough to recall the attack on the offices of
the satirical magazine *Charlie Hebdo*, where people
died just because they drew cartoons and believed in
free criticism and humour, even when it might offend
some people? Or the massacre in the Paris concert
venue Bataclan, where young people died, Muslims,
Christians, Jews and atheists, because they wanted to
go out and listen to music – in a club that had once
belonged to Jewish owners?[49] Or the slaughter on the

beach at Tunis, the indiscriminate killing of people who had gone there for recreation? Or the murder of a police officer and his partner in Magnanville? Is it not enough to know that Iraqi and Syrian Yazidis were kidnapped and tormented as sex slaves? That Iraqis and Syrians are pushed off high walls to their deaths just because they love differently or desire differently?[50]

Is the ideology important? The terror is that of a gang of criminals, resembling the cartels of the Mexican *narcotraficantes* in their brutality, in their practice of kidnapping and extortion, in their media communications aimed at spreading fear and terror, in the international scope of their activity. What purpose is served by examining the rhetoric of their programme? After the Paris attacks, President Barack Obama described the attackers as 'a bunch of killers with good social media'. Does it not border on trivializing their crimes to concern ourselves with whatever dogma this worldwide murder organization may spout?

Will McCants, one of the most knowledgeable analysts of IS and the director of the Project on US Relations with the Islamic World at the Brookings Institution, writes: 'Although I have studied jihadist culture for a decade, I am still astounded and dismayed by its ability to inspire individuals to take innocent life.'[51] We need some explanation of how people are being induced to kill others. How they are being trained to stop seeing others as human beings. What templates of hatred have to be prepared in order for them to torture and kill – without hesitation – children, women and men. How they are being trained to take the lives of other people, and to lose their own, supposedly for a higher goal – or for the like-minded audience that delights in their obscene spectacle of violence.

Occasionally, IS crimes are treated as if there were no longer anything surprising about them. The attacks are still unanimously condemned – but the amazement that people can be induced to murder so ruthlessly is dwindling. As if the sheer quantity of IS attacks had led to a certain inurement. As if it were enough to say, 'It was IS supporters', and that would automatically explain how people are schooled in this hatred, how they can be brought to regard other people as worthless. This peculiar attitude brings with it a danger of trivializing the violence, as if IS terror were something like a law of nature. As if Islamist terror were somehow automatic, and had no beginning.

But hatred and violence, including Islamist hatred and violence, do not simply appear out of nowhere. They are not a logical consequence 'of Islam'. They are not authentically Muslim. They are *made*. By a terrorist organization with a totalitarian ideology. Certainly the terror strategists also refer to Islamic texts – but Muslim scholars are almost unanimous in rejecting their pseudo-rigorist, violence-obsessed interpretation of the texts. In an open letter to IS supporters in 2015, 120 influential Muslim scholars criticized the ideology of IS as clearly *un-Islamic*. And it was by no means just a group of particularly liberal reformers who voiced their opposition to IS. The authors included the Grand Mufti of Egypt, Sheikh Shawqi Allam, as well as Sheikh Ahmad Al-Kubaisi, the founder of the Ulama Organization in Iraq. They included scholars from Chad, Nigeria, Sudan and Pakistan.[52] In their texts, the IS strategists manipulate their sources and their authorities to suit their purposes. They quote individual sentences without regard for the context in which they were written. They read and use isolated passages with no consideration for the whole textual setting. In their interpretations, they distort and pervert Islam – on this the Muslim scholars agree.

The violence of IS does not explode suddenly. The puppets who carry out IS actions, all the people who are manipulated into perpetrating suicide attacks or fighting in the war in Syria and Iraq, have to be indoctrinated in the visual regime which sees others only as enemies who can be killed with impunity. The patterns in which hatred pours out against women, against Jews, against homosexuals, against Shiites and all Muslims who are ostracized as apostates – these patterns are produced in countless texts and videos, in sermons and poems, and disseminated in conversations, on the net and in the street.

As I said at the beginning of this book, not just condemning hatred and violence, but examining how they function, always involves showing where something *else* would have been possible, where someone could have made a *different* decision, where someone could have *intervened*, where someone could have *opted out*. Not just rejecting hatred and violence, but observing what rhetorical strategies, what metaphors and images are used to generate and channel hatred, always goes hand in hand with the belief that we can identify those points in the narrative patterns at which the narrative can be interrupted or subverted.[53]

Some people argue that the IS phenomenon is not so much a radicalization of Islamists as an Islamization of radicals – but the people who take that view must still analyse how the terror network is able to recruit supporters from completely heterogeneous milieus and to mobilize them in the service of a nihilistic theology. Furthermore, studying the discursive and visual strategies of IS, its ideology and its self-image, is also the prerequisite for all police and military efforts to combat its terrorism. In confidential assessments, the commander of US special operations in the Near East, Major General Michael K. Nagata, addressed the problems of the fight against terrorism in 2014: 'We do not understand the movement, and until we do, we are not going to defeat it. We have not defeated the idea. We do not even understand the idea.'[54]

When it comes to drying up the pools in which hatred grows (and not just terrorism and organized violence), when it comes to identifying as early as possible the mechanics of exclusion, the processes of an increasingly radical thinking, everyone everywhere is called upon to join in the efforts to prevent fanaticism: social milieus, neighbourhoods, peer groups, families, online communities. Looking in this way at the structures that engender and channel hatred, the discourses which legitimize violence before it is committed and pay tribute to it afterwards, broadens the opportunities for engagement and action by civil society. In this perspective, resistance against fanaticism is not simply delegated to the security agencies, which have to intervene when the signs of possible crimes multiply. Defending an open, plural society in which religious and political and sexual diversity can prosper is everyone's duty.

*

The rise of IS must be situated in the historical and cultural context of recent political and social developments in Iraq and Syria. Nonetheless, we will examine IS here as a revolutionary-ideological renewal of the Salafist jihad. According to Fawaz A. Gerges of the London School of Economics, the world view of the Salafist jihad movement is essentially founded on and shaped by three documents or texts: first, the 286-page manifesto *The Management of Savagery* by Abu Bakr Naji, from the early 2000s; second, the *Introduction to the Jurisprudence of Jihad* by Abu Abdullah Muhajjer; and third, *The Essentials of Making Ready* by Sayyid Imam Sharif, alias Dr Fadl. Of the people who join IS or who profess adherence to it by their murderous acts, very few will have studied these documents. Nonetheless, they are tremendously informative in helping to understand how IS sees itself. Better-known sources no doubt include the few speeches by the leader Abu Bakr al-Baghdadi and the audio messages disseminated through various media by Abu Muhammad al-Adnani, the official spokesman of IS until his death in August 2016.[55] According to the *Die Zeit* journalist and terrorism expert Yassin Musharbash, the speeches of the founder of al-Qaida in Iraq, Abu Musab al-Zarqawi, are another well-known source.[56] Finally, there are elaborately conceived propaganda films which are particularly popular, such as the 36-minute film *Upon the Prophetic Methodology* from August 2014.[57]

In these documents, what kind of story does IS tell about itself? What kind of 'we' do they assert and invent – and how does the template of hatred take shape that motivates and enables people to torture and kill others? The first thing that stands out on reading the basic texts and speeches of IS is the promise of inclusion. In Abu Bakr al-Baghdadi's 2012 speech titled 'A Message to the Mujahidin and the Muslim Ummah in the Month of Ramadan', that promise takes the following form: 'You have a state and a caliphate [...] where the Arab and non-Arab, the white man and black man, the easterner and the westerner are all brothers.'[58] IS's contradictory self-concept identifies it as a state, but also as a potentially open territorial entity that does not respect the borders of existing nation-states.[59] IS creates a caliphate with an ostensibly flexible territory and open appeal, transcending existing nation-states. 'The Islamic State does not recognize synthetic borders nor any citizenship besides Islam.'[60] Thus al-Baghdadi in his 'Message to the Mujahidin' appeals to a clearly *transnational 'we'*. Arabs and non-Arabs, white and Black Muslims, from the East or the West, are to join together – in the fight against secularism, against idolatry, against 'the atheists' and 'the guards of the Jews'.

IS's hatred is, initially, an equalizer. Everyone – almost – is called upon to join the avant-garde of IS's jihad: young and old, men and women, from the neighbouring Arab states, from Chechnya, from Belgium, France and Germany; skin colour is unimportant, as is social background; they may be school drop-outs or A-Level students, officers from the former Iraqi army under Saddam Hussein or military amateurs.[61] Those who want to assimilate, who are willing to profess the doctrine propounded by al-Baghdadi, are welcome, and are promised the reward of ruling over others: 'Muslims will walk everywhere as a master.'[62]

The ideology of IS thus claims an ostensible openness to all who wish to join, and at the same time promises a superior status. Those who affirm allegiance to IS are supposed to become powerful, or at least free. All others are downgraded. Thus IS claims to be an *equalizer*, but at the same time presents itself as an *instrument of distinction*. IS members are supposed to be distinguished as a jihadist avant-garde with imperial ambitions whose goal is to revive (and impose by force) an 'original' form of Islam ascribed to the 'pious ancestors' (*as-salaf aṣ-ṣāliḥ*). Whether this genealogical reference to a medieval version of Islam is historically accurate, and not a completely modern invention, is debatable. More important is the rhetoric of a return to the past and the revival of an ostensibly 'true' Islam.[63]

At the same time, however, IS is explicitly a Sunni project. The Salafists denounce and despise Shia Islam as a categorical 'other'. Their vision is a paradoxical Sunni pan-Islamism, engaging in a hyper-Sunni identity politics while at the same time preaching a universal jihadism.[64] IS presents itself as both bounded and unbounded, as inclusive and exclusive – as an exclusive inclusion. The anthropologist Mary Douglas writes in her study on purity and danger: 'Pollution beliefs can be used in a dialogue of claims and counter-claims to status.'[65] With its cult of purity, IS tries to claim the supreme status for itself.

Its great attraction probably lies in exactly this dual promise: the unconditional invitation to belong to a timeless 'we', and at the same time to see oneself as a 'better', a 'true', an 'authentic' Muslim. That is the inclusive pull it exerts on all those Muslim Europeans who have no geographic feeling of belonging, and no sense of being part of a historic mission. An invitation to higher status may sound promising to people who are excluded, who are always treated as second-class citizens; to people who can see only empty words in the European promise of liberty, equality and fraternity; to people who live their lives in unemployment or in criminal milieus with no prospect of finding a job; to people who simply do not know what to do with themselves and their lives; to people in search of meaning or, failing that, some kind of excitement. They yield to the seduction of a simulated community in which all are allegedly welcome, although its organization is so anti-individualistic and authoritarian that every individual is ultimately robbed of his or her individuality. IS may promise individual glory, and devote media such as the online magazine *Dabiq* to recounting the personal stories of individual fighters and their military operations, but the IS regime ruthlessly punishes undesirable deviation or 'disloyalty'.[66]

Not only Christians and Jews are declared real or imagined opponents of this ultra-conservative project of radical purification, but also all those Muslims who are excluded from it by the accusation of apostasy. The manifesto *The Management of Savagery* defines IS's mission as freeing the community of Muslims from the 'degradation that afflicts it'. Not only 'the West' or the former colonial powers are blamed for the decline of Islam, but also all the distractions to which Muslims have succumbed. 'The power of the masses

[...] was tamed and its self-awareness was dissipated through thousands of diversions.'[67] The manifesto is full of contempt for all Muslims who allow themselves to be dissuaded from their duty to God. The factors that supposedly weaken the faithful include striving for wealth, 'the desires of the sexual organs and the stomach', and the 'deceptive media'. Whatever may keep Muslims from the pure worship of the One God is labelled decadent or 'filthy'. The order that IS wants to establish by violence is a rigorously pious order hygienically purified of all noxious passions.[68]

The narrative propagated by the texts to which IS refers is an apocalyptic one: the violence of the offensive jihad is supposed to escalate, qualitatively and strategically, in several stages. All chaos, all instability, is explicitly deemed advantageous on the path to the desired order of theocracy. The enemy is to be massacred and terrorized. Any clemency, any doubt about violence as the means of action, is despised as undue softness: 'If we are not violent in our jihad and if softness seizes us, that will be a major factor in the loss of the element of strength.'[69]

The world view is a dualistic one which admits only of absolute evil and absolute good. There is no middle ground, no nuance, no ambivalence. This is typical of all fundamentalists and fanatics: they tolerate no doubt of their own positions. Every thought, every argument, every quotation must be held as true and absolutely unambiguous. And this is a characteristic of authoritarian regimes: they leave no room for social or political dissent. It also explains why even the cruellest massacres, all the beheadings and burnings of prisoners, are accompanied by explanations and 'justifications'. That is perhaps the most surprising aspect of some of IS's execution videos: they seem remarkably 'didactic'; even the most brutal act, even the most unbearable exhibition of their contempt for human beings, is

given an 'educational' treatment and supplied with
'rationales'. Executions and the malicious destruction of
Shiite mosques or buildings are embedded in a narrative
that asserts their 'necessity'. Even in connection with
the most arbitrary violence, the impression that the
violence is arbitrary must be absolutely avoided. All
the indulgence in dramatization, all the sadistic joy in
tormenting people must be purged of the individual and
subjective factor. Every act on behalf of IS, the narrative
claims, must have a theologically explainable form,
a Salafist-jihadist 'reason'. A libidinous attitude to
violence, which is quite obviously present in some of the
perpetrators, is not sufficient: the violence must also be
charged with meaning. Not that the 'reasons' given are
logical. Their purpose, nonetheless, is to make hatred
and violence never seem random, but always purposeful
and controlled. Terror is presented as the logical terror
of an order whose legitimate authority is reflected in
every one of its acts. These constant self-explanations
have dual addressees and a dual message: outwardly,
they signal that the acts are not those of a disorganized
guerrilla, but of a powerful, legitimate state whose
communications attest to its mastery of technology
and the aesthetics of popular culture. At the same time,
they signal internally that no space will be allowed for
autonomous decisions, to say nothing of democratic
ambitions. The uninterrupted flow of communication
also imposes a hegemonic discourse which constantly
proclaims the totalitarian rule of IS.

*

IS pursues its ideological *cult of purity* not only on a
vertical axis, but also on a horizontal one. As I have
described, IS situates its rigorous programme in a plane
of theology and genealogy: it recalls (or rather invents)
the practices and beliefs of the 'ancestors' as models for

emulation in the present. At the same time, however, the demand of purification is also directed at the culturally hybrid societies of today, both in Arab countries and in Europe. The categorical others, the polluted and impure, include not only the supposedly apostate, corrupt distortions of Islam, but most of all the Enlightened modern age with its conception of a secular state permitting a diversity of religions and cultures. For the dogma of IS, that is the real *absolute other*: pluralism, coexistence in religious diversity, a state whose foundations are independent of any particular religion, and indeed resolutely secular.

A message by the former IS leader Abu Omar al-Baghdadi from 2007, 'Say I Am on Clear Proof from My Lord', announces, 'We believe that secularism despite the differences in its flags and parties [...] is a clear disbelief, opposing to Islam, and he who practices it is not a Muslim.'[70] This is an interesting passage. IS must declare secularism to be unbelief, something which is allegedly opposed to Islam. But secularism is not a religion. And it is noteworthy that IS nonetheless feels it must explicitly deny this. Indeed, the former leader of IS emphasizes that the 'practice of secularism' is un-Islamic and improper for Muslims. That sounds as if secularism were a specific practice. As if secularism required ritual prayer or pilgrimage. That is odd, since secularism refers to the constitution of a state which conceives its authority as explicitly post-metaphysical and divorced from all clerical power.

The ideology of purity does not allow the possibility of different religious beliefs and practices existing side by side. Nor that of a state conceiving of itself as enlightened and encompassing everyone equally, regardless of any particular religious confession, nor a society adopting a democratic, secular order in which everyone has equal subjective rights, everyone is entitled to pursue their particular religious practices and beliefs, everyone is accorded the same dignity. Nothing seems to be more abhorrent to IS than cultural or religious mixing. Anything hybrid, any plurality, stands in contradiction to this fetishism of purity. In this regard, the fanatical ideology of IS resembles that of the new right in Europe: they both identify the culturally 'impure', the peaceful coexistence of different faiths, as antagonistic. For Islam to be a part of Europe, for Muslims to be recognized in the open democracies of Europe just like members of other faiths (or of none) who respect the given constitution – to IS, that is both unthinkable and unwelcome.

This explains why IS actively spread propaganda against the German chancellor Angela Merkel's policy in the course of the humanitarian crisis of the Middle Eastern refugees and their reception in Europe. In at least five video messages, IS warned the refugees not to go to Europe.[71] These messages sharply criticized Muslims who live side by side with Jews, Christians and 'unbelievers'. The suggestions of right-wing agitators notwithstanding, the humanitarian gesture towards the refugees does not imply support for IS: on the contrary, every gesture, every law, every act that offers Muslim refugees a fair procedure, an open welcome, a real chance for inclusion in Europe, is a direct threat to the Islamist ideology. The use of refugee routes by IS to send potential attackers into Europe is a danger that must not be underestimated where police tactics and security policies are concerned. But that does not change the fact that the programmatic and military strategy driving IS's attacks and propaganda is aimed entirely at nurturing polarization in Europe. Dividing Europe into a Muslim and a non-Muslim society is an explicit milestone objective of the jihad. With every attack in Europe or the US, IS hopes, in its perverse but rigid rationality, that the target country will respond with a collective punishment of its Muslim population.

IS wants to see Muslims in the modern secular states placed under a blanket suspicion, isolated and ostracized – because only then can they be turned away and separated from the modern democracies and driven into the arms of IS. Every voice raised to condemn all Muslims after an Islamist terror attack, every voice that challenges Muslims' fundamental rights or their dignity, every voice that tries to associate Muslims only with violence and terror, fulfils the Islamist dream of a divided Europe, and unwittingly pays homage to the Islamists' cult of purity.

Hence it is critical for an enlightened Europe to persist in our commitment to the secular, open modern society. It will be imperative not only to tolerate cultural and religious and sexual diversity, but to celebrate them. Only in diversity does individual freedom flourish, not just for majorities, but also for nonconformists and dissenters. Only a liberal public sphere preserves space for dissent, for self-doubt – and for irony as the genre of ambiguity.

3

In Praise of the Impure

'But a "we" is not the adding together or juxtaposition of these "I"s.'

Jean-Luc Nancy, 'Being Singular Plural'

In the twenty-eight volumes of the *Encyclopédie*, the compendium of knowledge of the Enlightenment published between 1752 and 1772 by Denis Diderot and Jean-Baptiste Le Rond d'Alembert, there is a definition of 'fanaticism' which is still valid today. 'Fanaticism is a blind and passionate zeal,' according to the entry by Alexandre Deleyre, 'which originates from superstitious opinions and causes people to commit ridiculous, unjust, and cruel acts, not only shamelessly and ruthlessly, but with a kind of joy and consolation.'[1] This is what present-day fanatics have in common, both the pseudo-religious and the political zealots: they concoct dogmas and superstitions to kindle and 'justify' hatred. Shamelessly and ruthlessly, they sometimes merely advocate ridiculous positions, and sometimes commit unjust and cruel acts. Sometimes their blind propagation of the most absurd conspiracy theories seems rather amusing. But the humour soon pales when that superstition bolsters a doctrine that actually mobilizes people. When people incite hatred to intimidate, denounce and stigmatize other people, to deny them public space and speech, to attack and injure them – that is anything but amusing and ridiculous. Whether the fanaticism is linked to the notion of a homogeneous nation, a racist concept of belonging to a 'people' in an ethnic sense, or whether it is linked to a pseudo-religious idea of 'purity', all these doctrines share the illiberal mechanisms of arbitrary and intentional inclusion and exclusion.

If there is one thing that fanatics are dependent on in their dogmatism, it is univocal terms. They need a pure doctrine of a 'homogeneous' people, a 'true' religion, an 'original' tradition, a 'natural' family and an 'authentic' culture. They need passwords and codes that admit no objection, no ambiguity, no ambivalence – and that is where their greatest weakness lies. The dogma of the pure and the simple cannot be fought by mimetic adaptation. It is hopeless to fight rigorism with rigorism, fanaticism with fanaticism, to confront the haters with hatred. The enemies of democracy can be fought only by democratic means, with the rule of law. If the liberal, open society would defend itself, it can do so only by remaining liberal and open. If the modern, secular, pluralistic Europe is under attack, then it must not cease being modern, secular and pluralistic. If religious and/or racist fanaticism is driving a campaign to divide society into categories of identity and difference, then what is necessary are alliances and thinking in similarities. If fanatical ideologues present their world view only in crude simplifications, then the answer cannot be to surpass them in simplicity and crudeness; what is needed is discernment and nuance.

That means not rebutting the fanatics' essentialism with essentialist accusations. For this reason, criticism of and resistance against hatred and contempt should always be aimed, not at persons, but at the structures and conditions of hatred and contempt. The goal is not to demonize haters as human beings, but to criticize or prevent their verbal and non-verbal acts. And if those acts are crimes, then of course the perpetrators must be prosecuted. But in order to confront hatred and the fanaticism of purity, civil (and civilian) resistance is necessary against the techniques of exclusion and inclusion, against the templates of perception that make some people visible and others invisible, against the visual regimes that allow individuals to be seen only as representing groups. Courageous objection is necessary against all the mean little forms of humiliation, and so are laws and practices of support and solidarity with the persons being excluded. Different narratives are necessary: narratives in which different perspectives and different people become visible. Only when the patterns of hatred are replaced, only 'when we discover similarities where we only saw differences before'[2] – only then can empathy arise.

We must resist fanaticism and racism not only in substance, but also in form. That means *not* becoming radicalized ourselves. That means *not* nurturing the fantasy of a civil war or an apocalypse by practising hatred and violence. What is needed instead is economic and social intervention in the places and in the structures in which the dissatisfaction that is being diverted into hatred and violence first arises. A person who wants to take preventive action against fanaticism cannot avoid asking what social and economic insecurities are being masked behind the false certainties of pseudo-religious or nationalistic dogmas. A person who wants to take preventive action against fanaticism must ask why so many people value their lives so little that they are willing to give them up for an ideology.

But most of all, what is needed is a vindication of the impure and the complex, because that is what confounds the haters and the fanatics the most in their fetishism of the pure and simple. What is needed is a culture of enlightened doubt and irony – because those are the genres of thinking that are most inimical to the rigorist fanatics and racist dogmatists. Such an apologia for the impure must be more than an empty promise. What is needed is not just proclamations of plurality in European societies, but serious political, economic and cultural investments in such an inclusive community. But why? What is so precious about plurality? Is that not just setting one doctrine in place of another? What does plurality mean for those who fear that cultural or religious diversity will limit them in their own practices and beliefs?

'Men in the plural,' Hannah Arendt wrote in 1958 in *The Human Condition*, 'that is, men in so far as they live and move and act in this world, can experience meaningfulness only because they can talk with and make sense to each other and to themselves.'[3] Plurality, Arendt tells us, is first and foremost an inescapable empirical fact. No human being exists alone and in isolation; we live in the world in numbers – that is, in the plural. Yet plurality in the modern era does not mean the proliferation of an original model, a specified norm to which all others must assimilate. Rather, the *condition humaine* and human action are characterized, Arendt writes, by that plurality in which 'we are all the same, that is, human, in such a way that nobody is ever the same as anyone else who ever lived, lives or will live'.[4] This description elegantly contradicts the widely held conception of identity and difference. Arendt sees all human beings rather as belonging to the universal 'we' and at the same time as unique, distinctive individuals. The plural referred to here is not a static 'we', a compulsively self-homogenizing mass. In the tradition of Hannah Arendt, the plural is formed rather of the diversity of distinctive individuals. All of them resemble one another, but none is the same as any other – this is the remarkable and fascinating condition and potential of plurality. Any normalization that involves purging the singularity of individual human beings is in contradiction to such a concept of plurality.

Jean-Luc Nancy writes: 'The singular is primarily each one and, therefore, also with and among all the others.'[5] Singular thus does not mean egoistically individual. And plural does not mean 'the adding together or juxtaposition of these "I"s'. Individuality is discernible and realizable only in coexistence and cooperation. Alone, a person is not unique; he or she is merely alone. The individual needs the social collective which reflects or refracts her or his desires and needs. A 'we' that defines itself only as a monochromatic unity contains neither diversity nor individuality. In other words, cultural or religious diversity, a heterogeneous society, a secular state that creates the conditions and structures in which different life plans can exist side by side, equally, does not limit individual beliefs – on the contrary, it is what permits and protects them. *Plurality in a society does not mean the loss of individual (or collective) freedom; it is what ensures freedom.*

Pseudo-religious fanatics and ethnic nationalists like to paint a different picture: they demand a homogeneous, original, pure collective, suggesting that it would offer more protection or greater stability. They claim that a plural society endangers cohesion and subverts a tradition they revere. To this we may object, first, that the idea of a secular state is also traditional: it belongs to the tradition of the Enlightenment. Furthermore, traditions are not given, they are *made*. And, second, that the doctrine of a pure, homogeneous nation is no guarantee of stability, because it starts by segregating out everything that is declared 'foreign' or 'hostile' or 'false'. The concept of community that is founded on essentialism is the one which offers no protection. Only a liberal society that identifies itself as open and plural – one that imposes no standards in regard to religious or atheistic life plans – protects individually diverging beliefs or bodies, protects anomalous ideas and practices of the good life, love or happiness. This is not just a rational or normative argument, although it is often called that. Rather, the praise of the impure speaks to the affective needs of human beings as vulnerable beings and as beings susceptible to insecurity. Recognizing the cultural diversity of a modern society does not mean that individual life plans, individual traditions or religious beliefs would have no place in it. Recognizing a globalized reality does not mean being disrespectful towards individual conceptions of the good life.

For my part, I find cultural or religious or sexual differences in a secular legal system *reassuring*. As long as I see these differences in the public space, I know that free spaces are granted in which I too am protected as an individual with all my distinctive characteristics, my longings, my possibly diverging beliefs or practices. I feel less vulnerable when I notice that the society I live in permits and bears with different life plans, different religious or political beliefs. For that reason, I am also reassured by those ways of living or forms of expression that are far removed from my own. They do not annoy me. They do not scare me. On the contrary: I am glad of all kinds of rituals and festivals, practices and habits. Whether people get their enjoyment in marching bands or at the Wagner festival in Bayreuth, in the F.C. Union stadium in old East Berlin or at the 'Pansy Presents Drag Race' in the West; whether they believe in the Immaculate Conception or in the parting of the Red Sea, whether they wear a yarmulke or lederhosen or drag – respecting the lived diversity of others protects not only their individuality, but mine as well. In that sense, the praise of impurity is not merely a 'reasoned', rationalistic doctrine for a pluralistically constituted secular society – the frequently repeated argument notwithstanding. On the contrary, the affective advantages appear to me to be central: cultural or religious or sexual diversity means a gain, not a loss, in feelings of belonging and emotional stability. The social cohesion of an open, liberal society is no less strong than that of a closed, monocultural province. The affective bond is precisely to this: living in a society that defends and protects my individual characteristics, even if they will never appeal to the majority, even if they are old-fashioned, new-fashioned, quirky or tasteless. A society that explicitly defines itself as open and inclusive – and constantly examines self-critically whether it really lives up to that definition to a sufficient degree – a society like that fosters trust that I will not be arbitrarily ostracized or attacked.

Really existing in the plural means mutually respecting everyone's individuality and uniqueness. I do not have to live or think exactly as everyone else does. I do not have to share the practices and beliefs of others. I do not have to like them or understand them. This too is an aspect of the enormous freedom of a truly open, liberal society: not having to like one another, and yet being able to let one another be. And that explicitly includes those religious notions that some people may find irrational or incomprehensible. The subjective freedoms explicitly include devoutly religious life plans, which are perhaps as divergent from the majority in an open society as less traditional or atheistic ones. The concept of a secular state does not mean mandatory atheism for all citizens. The critical point is simply this: the less essentialist, the less homogeneous, the less 'pure' a society's conception of itself, the less compulsion there is for individuals to clump together in an identitarian mass.

We have begun to forget; the vocabulary of an inclusive, open society has been increasingly eroded or superseded. Today we have to spell out what it can and should mean *to exist in the plural*. If we want our coexistence to make sense – and not just to people who eat pork, but to everyone – then we have to find a language, and practices and images, for this plurality. Not just for those who have always been visible and welcome, but also for the others whose experiences or points of view are often silently overlooked.

Will there be conflicts in such a plural society? Yes, certainly. Will there be differences between cultural or religious sensitivities? Yes, of course. But there are no universal formulas to resolve these conflicts between religious requirements and the compromises that a secular, plural society demands from believers. Instead, every conflict over every practice must be examined and weighed individually: why is this ritual, this practice, important for a given religion? Whose rights could be violated or denied by it? Does it involve the use of force against a person? By what right can such a practice be prohibited? The grounds on which religious practices can prevail in the public spaces of a secular society, and the grounds on which they can be restricted or prohibited, are the subject of complex philosophical and legal debates. Public discussion is urgently called for on the question of limits to the freedom of religion and the relationship between secularism and democracy. Yes, this is hard work, and there will be legal prohibitions against certain practices or rituals which are incompatible with the constitution – such as forced marriages of minors. But these processes of negotiation are at the core of a democratic culture. They do not endanger democracy; they affirm it as a process of learning through deliberation and experience. That requires of every single believer, in addition to the commitment to his or her faith, a commitment to the secular, plural society. It requires that every single believer also learns to distinguish between individual values, which cannot be generalized, and constitutional norms, which apply to all, regardless of their faith or beliefs. It also requires that the secular society examines how secular it really is – whether some of its institutions and laws do not oddly prefer certain believers or certain churches. All that is required to endure these conflicts between different practices and different legal philosophies, and to negotiate implementations, is a certain amount of confidence in the processes of a democracy.

A democratic society is a dynamic, learning organization, and that implies an individual and collective willingness to admit individual or collective mistakes, to correct historical injustices and to forgive one another. A democracy is not simply a dictatorship of the majority; it defines a process in which people not only decide and elect, but also jointly discuss and deliberate. It is an organization which must and can be adjusted again and again wherever it is found to be insufficiently just or insufficiently inclusive. That requires a culture of addressing mistakes, a culture of public discussion which is characterized not by mutual contempt, but by mutual curiosity. Recognizing mistakes in our own thinking and actions is elementary for individuals and organizations in politics just as in the media and civil society. Mutually forgiving one another on occasion – that too is part of the moral fibre of a living democracy. Unfortunately, the structural conditions and the social habits of communication, especially in social media, are increasingly hindering a culture of discussion in which it is possible to admit mistakes or to forgive one another.

In her Frankfurt Lecture on Poetics, the writer Ingeborg Bachmann mentioned a way of thinking 'which initially is not concerned with its direction, a thinking that wants knowledge and wants to attain, with language and through language, something which we may tentatively call reality'.[6] We might similarly imagine a democratic public space and culture in which the direction is not always predetermined or known

ahead of time – in which people can and must think and
debate openly and self-critically. This kind of thinking,
which is not initially concerned with which way it will
lead, becomes more daunting as public debate becomes
more polarized and unbridled. But such a search for
knowledge is exactly what is needed: precisely this
search for the facts, for those descriptions of reality
which are not pre-filtered by ideological resentments.
And every person can and must join in this search.
There is no specific expertise in democracy. The philosopher Martin Saar writes: 'Everyone knows political
freedom and the democratic desire for freedom, even
those who are denied it.'[7]

*

Certainly it will also be difficult to bring together the
different historical and political experiences and memories
of people from different countries. That is a potential
source of conflict which cannot be disregarded. It will
be essential to give new explanations and new justifications for certain moral and political axioms, such as the
cautionary remembrance in German society of the crimes
of the Nazi period. Persons who are not connected to the
Shoah by their own family history can and must share
these principles; immigrants must address this historical
reference, the horror of this country's history. In other
words, the remembrance cannot be simply decreed; an
explanation why it can and must be relevant to everyone
is also needed. Immigrants must be given the opportunity
to relate to this history politically and morally, to understand it as their own – without the personal or familial
entanglements of guilt and shame. This history belongs
to them too because they live here and are citizens. To
claim an exemption from reflection on the Shoah would
imply an exclusion from the political narrative and the
self-image of this democracy.

'There is no remembrance and no relation to history which is not inspired by a desire, hence by something pointing to the future', said the French art historian and philosopher Georges Didi-Huberman in an interview in the journal *Lettre International.*[8] We must be aware of this twofold perspective of remembrance: it looks to the past and at the same time towards the future. Only a remembrance which draws a forward-looking purpose from the terrible legacy of history can remain effective and alive. Only a commemorative culture which gives new expression, over and over again, to the hope of creating an inclusive society, one which does not permit individuals or whole groups to be ostracized as 'foreign' or 'impure' – only such a culture of remembrance can remain vital. Only remembrance which remains attentive to the mechanisms of exclusion and violence in the present can avoid becoming meaningless someday.

But what if the historic experience being remembered and the present in which it is supposed to have a social and political purpose continue to move further and further apart? What if the eyewitnesses who remember personally and the people born later or elsewhere to whom they might recount their memories grow further and further apart? Not only in age, but also in what they recognize as familiar, what they experience and understand as theirs? How can the remembrance of the crimes of Nazi fascism be kept alive in the future without being reduced to something static? These questions most urgently beset Jews – but they concern everyone in our society. These questions have not come up only since the Syrian refugees provoked a more conscious reflection on the moral grammar of an immigrant society. They are also raised by the revanchist slogans of right-wing populist movements and by the public, physical attacks on Jews. It does not imply a blanket suspicion of anti-Semitism among Syrians or Saxons to ask how a commemorative culture can be communicated to people who did not grow up with it, or who perceive it only as imposed by decree.

Of course, with the Syrian refugees, we also encounter other experiences and other perspectives on the state of Israel. There is less familiarity with what the history of the Holocaust means, what pain and what trauma, than we take for granted in Germany. That will lead to confusion and misunderstanding. And it will be necessary to explain the crimes that were committed here, and the legacy and the obligation they represent for subsequent generations. The remembrance of Auschwitz has no half-life. It will therefore be necessary to narrate this history, with more modern didactic methods, as one that people can receive with curiosity and empathy. The many wonderful examples from the programmes of museums and cultural institutions have long since demonstrated that it is possible to inspire younger people to engage both creatively and seriously with the history of the Nazi period. This work must be supported more strongly than it has been up to now to develop formats especially for people who approach this history with different cultural and historical references.

That requires not only remaining aware of the special depth of guilt incurred in the past, but also attentively listening in the present to discover what injuries the refugees tell of and what memories their narratives hold. It will not work if we do not listen to one another. It cannot succeed if refugees do not have the opportunity to speak too of their memories, their fears. Listening does not mean agreeing with everything we hear. It only means wanting to understand where the other person comes from and what standpoint engenders their different perspective. We will demonstrate who we want to be as a society by our ability to conduct such an open narrative of multiple times and voices. And we will show who we want to be as a society by our ability

Against Hate

to anchor such an open, polyphonic narrative upon secular axioms of human rights.[9]

But this challenge is not new. Reflecting on the experience of historical guilt and thinking about the suffering and the perspectives of people who have been subjected elsewhere to extreme disenfranchisement and abuse, violence and war is something which comes up again and again in a society of immigrants. German memory has long included the experiences and perspectives of different people and groups from the formerly Yugoslavian countries; German memory has long included the experiences and perspectives of different people and groups from Turkey, the Kurdish areas, Armenia, and many other regions. German memory has long included the postcolonial experiences and perspectives of Black Germans. Existing in the plural means, first of all, recognizing these different memories and experiences and accepting their public articulation and negotiation. Existing in the plural means not just declaring ourselves – reluctantly, after decades of migration – a 'country of immigrants'. It also entails comprehending what it actually means to *be* a country of immigrants. The days when migrants and their children and grandchildren were admitted only as objects in public discourse are gone for good. It is time we understood that the migrants, the refugees, who have come here also participate in public discourses as subjects. That calls for a *pluralization of perspectives*, a critical examination of the templates of perception and the canon of knowledge that propagates cultural practices and beliefs. Existing in the plural will also mean taking seriously the knowledge that has been considered less important because it came later. In school curricula, this knowledge, these perspectives, have been undervalued up to now. The history of the literature, art and culture of both European and non-European societies is astonishingly neglected in educational institutions.[10] The narrow school canon has not kept pace sufficiently with the demands of a globalized world and the reality of life in a society of immigrants. There are isolated exceptions to this narrow vision: there are instances of schools and teachers who take on other materials and other authors – but, so far, not enough. It is not a matter of retiring Büchner and Wieland, but of reading something by Orhan Pamuk or Dany Laferrière or Terézia Mora or Slavenka Drakulić for a change. Such texts are not only elementary for children of migrant families, who may be able to recognize in them the experiential worlds of their parents and grandparents and see them valued. That is important, of course. But, primarily, they are relevant for the other children, who can learn to imagine and to discover a new world besides the obvious and familiar one. Such reading is an exercise in changing perspectives and in empathy.

The pluralization of perspectives should also go further in government agencies and state institutions: the police, the city halls, the courts. There have already been some tangible efforts to achieve more diversity in this sector. That is a good thing. Visible diversity in institutions and in enterprises is not just political cosmetics; it generates among younger people a whole different vision of what they can grow up to be. Visible diversity pluralizes the role models that give others orientation. Government agencies and state institutions reflect the self-image of a society: this is where they signal who is qualified and permitted to represent the state – who fully belongs to the society. The more diverse the staff of government agencies, the more credible the democratic promise of recognition and equality.

In his 1983 lectures at the Collège de France, published as *The Government of Self and Others*, the French philosopher Michel Foucault developed the idea of 'truth-telling' (*dire-vrai*), based on the Greek concept of *parrhesia*.[11] The superficial definition of parrhesia is simply free speech. But, for Foucault, parrhesia denotes that truth-telling which criticizes powerful opinions or positions. What Foucault is interested in is not only the content of what is said – that is, the fact that someone is telling the truth – but rather in the *way* in which things are said: this is what characterizes parrhesia. Truth-telling, in Foucault's conception, has certain prerequisites. It is not enough just to *name* the truth; parrhesia also requires actually *meaning* it. I do not simply make a true statement; I also *believe* that it is true. Parrhesia is not compatible with a manipulative or deceptive intention. It is not only true as a statement, but also honest. This sets it apart from the kind of dishonest pretence that is often heard today from nationalistic movements and right-wing populist parties: they say they have nothing against Muslims, *but* ...; they say they do not want to abridge the right to asylum, *but* ...; they say they reject hatred and violence, *but* they must be permitted to say .... This is not truth-telling.

Furthermore, truth-telling has to do with a certain constellation of power. The truth-teller is someone who, in Foucault's words, 'stands up to a tyrant and tells him the truth'.[12] Thus truth-telling always refers to words which the speaker lacks the right or the status to speak; it is speech in which the speaker takes a *risk*. Today we have no tyrants in the classical sense, but truth-telling is nonetheless needed. Eric Garner's sentence, 'This stops today', illustrates how such truth-telling can sound in our time. It requires the courage to stand up for oneself or for others who are denied the right or the status of belonging. The parrhesia that is called for in the public space today is directed against the powerful apparatus of explicit and implicit norms, against the patterns of hatred that degrade and denounce migrants, against the visual regimes that overlook Black people as if they were not human beings of flesh and blood, against the constant suspicion of Muslims, against the mechanisms and habits that disadvantage women, and against the laws that deprive gay and lesbian, bisexual and trans persons of the chance to marry and start families as other people do. It is directed against all the techniques of exclusion and contempt with which Jews are being isolated and stigmatized once again. Present-day truth-telling is also directed against the templates of perception and the visual regimes that make people who are forced to live in socially precarious conditions invisible: people who are excluded, not because of their religious or cultural beliefs, but simply because they are poor or unemployed. They are neglected in a society which still defines worth by work, even though everyone knows that mass unemployment is a structural constant. In their name too, and for their visibility, truth-telling is needed against the taboo of social class: it is not just specific people who are stigmatized as politically or socially 'redundant'. The category of social class is simply ignored today, as if it no longer existed. While many are marked and excluded as categorically 'other', poor and unemployed people are sometimes treated as if they did not exist as a group. This denial of social inequalities leads people who live in precarious conditions and poverty to feel that their situation is individual and their own fault.

The Israeli sociologist Eva Illouz has pointed out that truth-telling is not necessarily aimed in just one direction or directed to a single addressee. There have been historical situations in which a person has been obliged to speak up against several constellations of power at the same time.[13] That is to say, truth-telling may well be directed not only against the state and its discourses of exclusion, not only against powerful movements and parties, but also against one's own social milieu: against one's family, one's circle of friends, one's religious community, the political context in which one moves – and in which courageous protest may also be necessary against exclusive codes and complacent resentments. That requires not simply taking up a position of real or imaginary victimhood, taking on the role of a marginalized community, but watching out within one's own group for any condensation of excluding and stigmatizing dogmas or practices, whether individual or collective. Watching out for the formation of any patterns of perception in which hatred and contempt can find expression. Here too, Illouz writes, a universalist protest is called for.

Foucault's description of parrhesia offers a clue to how resistance against hatred and fanaticism should be expressed. People who are being denied their subjectivity, whose skin, bodies, privacy are not respected, who are categorized not as human beings – as equals – but as 'antisocial', as 'unproductive' or 'unworthy', those people who are categorized as 'perverse', as 'criminal', as 'sick', as ethnically or religiously 'impure' or 'unnatural', and in this way dehumanized – all of them must be reincorporated as individuals in a *universal 'we'*.

That means we must disconnect all the links, all the chains formed of associations, the conceptual or metaphorical distortions and stigmas that have been rehearsed over years and decades; we must penetrate the templates of perception, the patterns in which individuals are bound to groups and the groups to properties and pejorative attributions. 'Social conflicts are choreographed along the lines of narrative fields', writes Albrecht Koschorke in *Fact and Fiction*. In his terms, we must defeat that choreography by our words and our acts.[14] The patterns of hatred described in the first part of this essay are shaped in narratives that portray an especially narrow view of reality. Individuals or whole groups are seen only in connection with disparaging properties: they are thought of as 'foreign', 'different', 'lazy', 'animal', 'morally corrupt', 'inscrutable', 'disloyal', 'promiscuous', 'dishonest', 'aggressive', 'sick', 'perverse', 'oversexed', 'frigid', 'unbelieving', 'godless', 'dishonourable', 'sinful', 'contagious', 'degenerate', 'antisocial', 'unpatriotic', 'unmanly', 'unfeminine', 'seditious', 'suspected terrorists', 'criminal', 'bitchy', 'dirty', 'slutty', 'weak', 'spineless', 'zealous', 'seductive', 'manipulative', 'greedy', and so on.

In this way, the constantly repeated chains of association crystallize into supposed certainties. They implant themselves in media representations; they solidify in fictional formats, in stories or films; they are reproduced online and in institutions – in schools, for example, when teachers are asked to recommend which students are 'university bound' and which are not. They condense in intuitive or not-so-intuitive practices of ID checks and searches; they materialize in the selection processes in which certain applicants for advertised positions are less likely to be invited to interviews.

Lack of imagination is a powerful antagonist of justice and emancipation – and the truth-telling that is needed is one which *broadens* the scope of the imagination. Spaces of social and political participation, spaces of democratic action begin with the discourses and the images in which we address and recognize people. The complexity that we must set against the fanatical dogmas of the simple and the pure begins precisely here, in a return to precise observation to counter the fantastical conspiracy theories, the collective attributions, the crude generalizations of ideological resentments. 'Observing carefully means taking apart', writes Herta Müller – and so we must take apart and dissolve the templates of perception that constrict reality. We need to dismantle the false generalizations in which individuals are arrested simply as representatives of a whole group, so that individual persons and their acts become discernible again. And we must subvert and transform the slogans and designations that exclude and include.

The practice of resignifying – that is, assimilating and reinterpreting stigmatizing terms and practices – has a long history, and continuing that tradition can surely be called a poetic technique of resistance against hatred and contempt. The African American civil rights movement and the later emancipation movement of gay, lesbian, bisexual, transgender and queer people are full of examples of such ironic, performative resignification practices. Today, the performance format of the 'Hate Poetry Slam' is such an example, constituting a creative and hilarious variant of truth-telling against hatred and contempt.[15] There are other ways to confound the powerful attributions and stigmas. There are catalogues of specific measures for confronting hatred more effectively, especially in its echo chambers on social media. All of these instruments are necessary: social and artistic interference, public debates and discussions, political education and training events, and laws and ordinances.

Foucault refers to another aspect of parrhesia, truth-telling: it is not only aimed at (and 'throws the truth in the face of') a powerful, tyrannical recipient, but is also aimed reflexively at the speaker. I like that very much. As if in truth-telling one could mutter to oneself, make a pact with oneself. Truth-telling against powerful injustice is always a kind of alliance of the truth-teller with herself or himself: in stating the social and political truth, I feel myself bound by it and to it. Yet this courageous act of truth-telling, Foucault emphasizes, brings with it more than just a duty. It also binds the speaker to the *freedom* which is apparent in and realized in truth-telling. As an act of freedom, truth-telling against injustice is a gift, for it sets the truth-teller in a relation to themselves which opposes the alienating effect of power, its mechanisms of exclusion and stigma. For this reason, truth-telling can never be a unique act, a singular choice: its pact has a permanent effect, obligating the speaking subject.

Those who know this best are probably the countless people who volunteered to help refugees during the humanitarian crisis in Europe. It may seem surprising at first glance to interpret this voluntary service as a form of speaking truth to power. But the countless willing citizens, young people and older people, all the families who took refugees into their homes, the police officers and fire-fighters who worked extra shifts, all the school and kindergarten teachers who volunteered for 'welcoming classes', everyone who gave their time or food or shelter – all of them flouted social expectations and bureaucratic rules. They were not content simply to delegate the task of caring for refugees to state or local agencies. Rather, they filled the political vacuum that existed in many places with the dissenting, generous commitment of a tremendously heterogeneous social movement. That was not easy; it is not always easy. It takes time as well as strength and courage. For, just as any encounter with refugees always carries the potential of discovering something that delights and enriches us, every such encounter also holds the potential of discovering something we do not understand, something we are averse to, something disturbing.

For me, this service counts as a version of truth-telling because it takes place in spite of increasing pressure from the street, sometimes including considerable hostility and threats. Guards are still needed in front of refugee shelters; volunteers are still subjected to insults and threats. It takes courage to oppose such hatred and not to be deterred from what one feels to be a humanitarian duty or a natural human response. Every attack, every rampage by a mentally ill or fanatically mobilized refugee brings additional pressure to bear on such dedication, and additional objections from third parties. It takes tremendous patience, as well as self-confidence, to continue caring for the people who need help and attention, people who must not be punished for the deeds of others.

To me, civil resistance against hatred also includes taking back the spaces of imagination. The dissenting strategies against resentment and contempt also include – and this may seem surprising after everything said up to now – the *stories of happiness*. In view of all the different instruments and structures of power that marginalize and disenfranchise people, resistance against hatred and contempt must include taking back the various ways of living a happy and truly free life. Contradicting the tyrant always involves resisting the repressive-productive violence of power. It also means not accepting the role of the oppressed, the disenfranchised, the desperate. Being stigmatized and excluded entails not just being restricted in one's capacity to act: all too often it robs one of the energy and the courage to demand something that seems normal to and is taken for granted by everyone else: not only the right to participation, but also the *imagination of happiness*.

For that reason, the strategies of dissent against exclusion and hatred also include telling stories of *successful dissenting lives and loves*, so that, besides all the narratives of misfortune and contempt, the *possibility of happiness* also takes hold as something that can exist for everyone, as a prospect which everyone is entitled to hope for: not just those who fit the dominant norm, not just those who are white, who can hear, who get around easily, who feel at home in the body they were born in, not just those whose desire is what the advertisements and the laws prescribe, those who have the 'right' faith, the 'right' papers, the 'right' CV, the 'right' gender – but everyone.

Truth-telling also means entering into a pact with the truth told. Not just believing that, even if all people are not the same, all people are *equal*, but spelling out that equality: really demanding it, constantly, against the pressure, against the hatred, until it gradually becomes *not just poetically imagined, but real.*

'Power is always, as we would say, a power potential and not an unchangeable, measurable, and reliable entity like force or strength', writes Hannah Arendt in *The Human Condition.* 'While strength is the natural quality of an individual seen in isolation, power springs up between men when they act together and vanishes the moment they disperse.'[16] That would also be the most apt and beautiful description of a 'we' in an open, democratic society: this 'we' is always a potential, not something immutable, measurable, reliable. No one defines the 'we' alone. It arises when people act together, and it disappears when they split apart. Rising up against hatred, joining together in a 'we', to speak with one another and act with one another: that would be a courageous, constructive and delicate form of power.

Postscript

While I was writing this book about hatred and resentment, the Brexit referendum had not yet taken place in the United Kingdom and Donald Trump was not yet President of the United States.

The dogma of purity with which the neo-nationalist movements and candidates propagated their policies was horribly familiar. The construction of a monstrous 'other' allegedly threatening an 'us'; the escapist narrative of a 'before' to which 'we' must return; the racist, chauvinist, obscurantist motifs – all of these are no longer marginal or taboo; they now dominate the discourse and the actions of the government in the White House.

The Brexit decision took me completely by surprise. I am still amazed at how the combination of magical thinking and unmagical lying succeeded in misleading the public. The campaign was dominated by animistic incantations and xenophobic curses promising a more autonomous and more authentic nation, free of 'foreign rule' by Europe. These promises spoke to a regressive nostalgia in a transnational present. Who wants to join together with other butterflies when you can feed yourself alone in caterpillar mode? This is how some of the protagonists sounded as they explained their vision of a shrinking nation.

The election of Donald Trump, on the other hand, did not surprise me. Maybe that had something to do with the fact that I had spent years travelling in the United States as a reporter for stories on the destruction in New Orleans after Hurricane Katrina, on the social upheavals after the financial crisis of 2008–9, on the paradoxes of the 'American Dream'; I had talked to undocumented migrants in Arizona, striking Walmart workers in Chicago, and the West Virginian families of torturing soldiers who served in Abu Ghraib. Anyone who has spoken with homeless veterans of the Afghanistan war living under highway bridges in Nevada, listened to dealers at gun shows in Mississippi who sell patches embroidered with the slogan 'Pork-eating Crusader' in English and Dari, or attended a worship service in a megachurch in Colorado cannot be surprised at the anger that Donald Trump was able to channel.

But a foreboding that something can happen does not lessen the grief when it does.

Authoritarian, antimodern, obscurantist regimes, whether in the US, Russia or Turkey, far-right or radical-evangelical movements, whether in Europe or Latin America, threaten not only the rights of those who are branded as 'other' because they have somewhat different looks, somewhat different beliefs, somewhat different desires from the norm. Such regimes and movements not only intensify the climate of fear for those who are already living precarious lives (such as the 'Dreamers' in America or the Windrush generation in Britain); they not only normalize and legitimize resentments and attacks against LGBTI persons, Muslims, Jews, refugees or people of colour; they not only demonize and criminalize the endeavours of international organizations working to spread and safeguard human and civil rights.

Not only that, but they also threaten and subvert all the institutions and laws that are public and shared by everyone. This objective is common to xenophobic and neoliberal agendas: they challenge the *res publica*; they undermine the spaces and values that are supposed to transcend individual inclinations and benefit everyone. It would never occur to the neo-nationalists that there are good reasons to finance or support something that does not reflect the interests of their own clan, their own social or cultural group, their own nation. The radical assault led by authoritarian, obscurantist movements and governments arises from a longing for social and religious fragmentation. That is why they oppose all those individuals, publishers and broadcasters who communicate a shared reality, who distinguish between evidence and allegation, knowledge and assumption, criticism and censorship, truth and fiction, investigation and stenography, journalism and lobbying.

The praise of the impure, the plea for a society that can and must be inclusive and diverse, is more necessary than ever. Dissent and protest are needed against all those who would rank human beings in hierarchies, with gradations between persons who are entitled to human rights and others who are not. Dissent and protest are needed against those who would dictate whose suffering counts and whose doesn't; whose skin, whose body, whose faith, whose dignity may be challenged; who may be humiliated or hurt, and who may not.

And for the sake of that dissent and protest, it is also necessary that we not let ourselves be divided. After Trump was elected, there were hasty attempts to deny that racism was a motivation: the broad alliance of white voters of all ages and social classes who had voted for Trump were reduced in retrospect by numerous commentators to the poor white working class. In this way, the election was reinterpreted as the legitimate expression of the justified concerns and interests of socially marginalized persons.

At the same time, there was an attempt to play off social and cultural identities against one another. Suddenly the forgotten white working class was pitted against the allegedly too dominant Blacks, LGBT persons, feminists and migrants: here the 'justified' social concerns of the nation's workers; there the 'secondary' cultural concerns of people marginalized for religious or sexual or racist reasons, whose hardships were dismissed as 'luxury problems'.

The dichotomy is absurd: as if poverty were not also stigmatized. And as if, conversely, religious or racist exclusion did not have economic consequences. As if Mexican workers in the United States or Jamaican workers in Great Britain, queer Muslims in Germany or Jewish pensioners in France did not have stories to tell of multiple discrimination and contempt. Social hardship and exclusion cannot be separated from one another. The issues of economic and cultural exclusion must be conceived and addressed together.

It will be crucial to reject hatred's invitation to adopt it for ourselves. Neo-nationalistic essentialism cannot be fought with essentialism. Those who allow themselves to be manoeuvred into using the rhetorical or political genres and instruments of the authoritarian, obscurantist movements, who think that populism can only be contested by a populism with a different identitarian charge, have already lost. It will be necessary to employ all the political genres that are abhorrent to the dogma of purity: poetic dissidence and irony are needed; artistic formats are just as necessary as legal complaints; political, social and aesthetic practices are needed to revitalize the vision of an inclusive, open, heterogeneous society.

This job will not be finished when the authoritarian and neo-nationalist regimes in various countries of the world have been replaced and the far-right parties have disappeared from the legislatures. A democracy is not something you have; it is not a completed project, not something you can ever be satisfied with. A democracy is always not-there-yet; it is imperfect, vulnerable, open to criticism, to change, to collective learning. Too much confidence is just as bad for a democracy as too little confidence. That is why a certain political melancholy is necessary, an affliction at insufficient emancipation, insufficient freedom, insufficient justice. And a kind of political desire is necessary, a resistant appetite for collective action, expanding together with others the spaces in which we can live, work, talk, love.

Notes

Preface

1 Among the powerful techniques of exclusion and stigmatization are the words used to designate people. To many who deal with issues of exclusion in academic or activist contexts, the politics of language and the debate on appropriate designations is a serious ethical problem. Even supposedly 'self-evident' categories such as 'black and white' only repeat the racist attributions and divisions they are trying to criticize. That is why there are a multitude of verbal strategies to deal with this problem more sensitively: from omitting and replacing the charged words to various creative forms of marking (such as writing 'white' in lower case and capitalizing 'Black' to reverse the social hierarchy). These political choices of diction are often far removed from common habits of speaking and writing, however. Of course, that is exactly the political intention: to change our habits. But, at the same time, it impairs their effectiveness in relation to the people they are supposed to influence. What is important to note, in any case, is that 'Black' and 'white', as they are used in this text, are by no means assertions of objective fact. They are attributions in a specific historical and cultural context. Who is read and seen as 'Black', for what reason and with what consequences, is the subject of formidable controversy.

Racism and the historically encumbered attributions are discussed at length in the section on Eric Garner at the end of Chapter 1.

2 Thus Giorgio Agamben describes the status of 'homo sacer' as a person outside the law. See Giorgio Agamben, *Homo Sacer: Sovereign Power and Bare Life*, trans. Daniel Heller-Roazen, Palo Alto: Stanford University Press, 2002, 71ff.

3 Just as a thought experiment, try to imagine this in reverse: of course we accept heterosexuality, but why must heterosexuals always be so flagrantly heterosexual? Of course they can love each other privately; that doesn't bother anybody; but why do they have to marry?

4 This book does not discuss individual pathologies or psychoses that may express themselves in hatred and violence (in mass shootings, for example). The question to what extent such psychological dispositions are especially exacerbated in times of political and ideological mobilizations of hatred would be the subject of a separate study.

1 Visible, Invisible

1 See also Axel Honneth's beautiful essay 'Invisibility: On the Epistemology of "Recognition"', *Aristotelian Society Supplementary Volume*, 75:1, 2003, 111–26.

2 Claudia Rankine, *Citizen*, Minneapolis: Graywolf, 2014, 17.

3 I tell this story not to recommend the practice, but as a further illustration of Shakespeare's notion of love as a temporary projection.

4 This distinction is also characterized as one between the object and the 'formal object' of an emotion. See William Lyons, *Emotion*, Cambridge: Cambridge University Press, 1980.

5 Martha Nussbaum, *Political Emotions: Why Love Matters for Justice*, Cambridge, MA: Harvard University Press, 2015, 182ff.

6 I have written at length about the passive model of identity developed by Jean-Paul Sartre, and later Iris Marion Young, in Carolin Emcke, *Kollektive Identitäten*

(Collective identities), Frankfurt am Main: Campus, 2000, 100–38. The degree to which it is actually applicable to different forms of fanaticism and specific fanatical groups requires a more detailed and specific investigation than I can undertake here.

7 Didier Eribon, *Returning to Reims*, trans. Michael Lucey, Los Angeles: Semiotext(e), 2013, 148.

8 Jürgen Werner, *Tagesrationen: Ein Alphabet des Lebens* (Daily rations: an alphabet of life), Frankfurt am Main: Tertium Datur, 2014, 220.

9 In the words of Jan-Werner Müller: 'This is the core claim of populism: only some of the people are really the people.' Jan-Werner Müller, *What is Populism?* Philadelphia: University of Pennsylvania Press, 2016, 21. In the German version of his book (*Was ist Populismus?* Berlin: Suhrkamp, 2015), Müller also asks what difference it would make if just one word were added to the slogan: 'We *too* are the people.'

10 Her reaction reminds me of a sentence in Frantz Fanon: 'After everything that has just been said, it is easy to understand why the first reaction of the black man is to say *no* to those who endeavour to define him.' Frantz Fanon, *Black Skin, White Masks*, trans. Richard Philcox, New York: Grove Press, 2008, 19.

11 Aurel Kolnai, *Ekel Hochmut Hass: Zur Phänomenologie feindlicher Gefühle* (Disgust, arrogance, hate: on the phenomenology of hostile feelings), Frankfurt am Main: Suhrkamp, 2007, 102.

12 Elaine Scarry, 'The Difficulty of Imagining Other Persons', in *Human Rights in Political Transitions: Gettysburg to Bosnia*, ed. Carla Hesse and Robert Post, New York: Zone, 1999, 288.

13 The only term that seems fitting to me would be 'pack', as used by Elias Canetti: 'The pack ... consists of a group of men in a state of excitement whose fiercest wish is to be more.' Elias Canetti, *Crowds and Power*, trans. Carol Stewart, New York: Farrar, Straus & Giroux, 1984 [1962], 93.

14 In German, *Döbeln wehrt sich – meine Stimme gegen Überfremdung*, https://www.facebook.com/

Döbeln-wehrt-sich-Meine-Stimme-gegen-Überfremdung
-687521988023812/photos_stream?ref=page_internal.

15 At the time of writing, these photos, videos and comments
were visible on the Facebook page.

16 Cathrin Reichelt, 'Autoliv schliesst Werk in Döbeln'
(Autoliv closes factory in Döbeln), *Sächsische Zeitung*,
22 August 2013, http://www.sz-online.de/sachsen/
autoliv-schliesst-Werk-in-doebeln-2646101.html.

17 The *ReiseGenuss* company's coach that was eventually
blockaded in Clausnitz started its trip that day in
Schneeberg, and stopped at the alien registration office
in Freiberg on its way to Clausnitz. It never stopped in
Döbeln.

18 Kolnai, *Ekel Hochmut Hass*, 132–3.

19 Max Horkheimer and Theodor W. Adorno, *Dialectic
of Enlightenment*, trans. Edmund Jephcott, Palo Alto:
Stanford University Press, 2002, 140.

20 Christoph Demmerling and Hilge Landweer, *Philosophie
der Gefühle* (Philosophy of emotions), Stuttgart: J. B.
Metzler, 2007, 296.

21 Thus Holger Münch, the head of the German
Federal Police Bureau, pronounced a remarkably
clear warning in June 2016: 'Words precede acts.'
'Die Sprache kommt vor der Tat' (Words precede
acts), interview, *Frankfurter Allgemeine Zeitung*,
4 June 2016, http://www.faz.net/aktuell/politik/inland/
bka-chef-muench-im-interview-die-sprache-kommt-
vor-der-tat-14268890.html.

22 Scarry, 'The Difficulty of Imagining Other Persons', 285.

23 The exhibition 'Sticky Messages', produced by the
Centre for Anti-Semitism Research and the German
Historical Museum, traces these historical lines running
from old prejudices and themes to the present-day
pictorial politics of anti-Semitic and racist stickers. In
the 1920s, the defamation campaign 'Black Disgrace'
(*Schwarze Schmach*) 'warned' of the alleged 'brutality'
of Black people; postage stamps depicted huge, dark
figures assailing defenceless white women's bodies. This
same racist insinuation of a sexual threat allegedly posed
by 'foreigners' is being repeated today.

24 What makes this historical quotation in a new environment so perfidious is the fact that it instrumentalizes the public awareness of sexual violence that has been achieved and channels it in a direction to serve hatred. In the present day, when sexual violence against children and women is criminalized, when it is no longer downplayed or belittled, the quotation links the illegitimate patterns of racist attributions (the stirred-up fear of 'aggressive foreigners' or 'Arab men') with the legitimate and necessary sensitivity towards sexual violence against children and women. That is why fomenting fear of 'child molesters' is such a popular rhetorical tool of the radical right: because it can generate agreement across a broad social spectrum. Of course everyone wants to oppose sexual violence. But in this context, the warning against sexual assault mainly serves to aggravate resentment against 'Arab men' or 'Black men'.

25 This is not by chance; it is the result of conscious rhetorical tactics. In a report broadcast on 14 May 1989 in the magazine programme *Spiegel TV*, the superficial polishing of racist ideology can be seen in action. A cameraman attends a cadre training course of the German ultranationalist party, the NPD. In a seminar, the students practise speaking on the subject of the 'foreigner problem'. The seminar is designed as a role-playing session: one participant gives a speech while the others are asked to play opponents or hecklers. The NPD student responds to the question whether there is a duty to aid foreigners from war zones by saying, 'Those are poor devils; of course they have to be helped. But it doesn't help them to try to integrate them here ... that's impossible. They're a different race with different characteristics, a different lifestyle....' In the subsequent feedback phase, the instructors offer tactical corrections: 'Then you say "races" ... that's another word I would never use in this context ... You meant "a different mentality." But that way [i.e., by saying 'race'], of course, you get the left or the [unintelligible] press ... "He's a racist."' The instructor's critique refers not to the implication that there is such a thing as different 'races',

and that certain properties can be collectively attributed to them; rather, the critique singles out the word 'race' only because it invites the accusation that the speaker is a racist. This kind of rhetorical training explains why the nationalists' discourse comes across so smoothly today – without having changed its ideological content at all. I thank Maria Gresz and Hartmut Lerner of the *Spiegel TV* documentary section for access to this feature.

26 In this milieu even the police are perceived, perhaps not as enemies, but at least as manipulated or confused. Appeals are directed at police officers, explaining to them whom they should support and whom they should protect. 'The people', they explain, are 'your family, your relatives, your friends, your neighbours.' The idea that police officers should primarily protect the rule of law and all the people living here, regardless of whether they are related or acquainted with them – that is apparently invalid.

27 In this uniform discourse, any attempt to make distinctions serves to confirm the blanket suspicion. For an example from the same context: a photo of a glass dish containing many-coloured M&Ms, with the line above it in big letters: 'Not all refugees are criminal or evil'; and below it, in smaller type: 'But imagine a dish of M&Ms in which 10% are poisoned. Would you eat a handful of them?'

28 Those discourses include publications, such as the far-right German magazine *Sezession*, which purport to be, or perhaps are, rational and intellectual, and yet which supply all the themes and interpretations necessary for hatred against the people in the coach. See also Liane Bednarz and Christoph Giesa, *Gefährliche Bürger: Die Neue Rechte greift nach der Mitte* ('Dangerous citizens: the new right pushes towards the centre'), Munich: Hanser, 2015; Volker Weiss, *Deutschlands neue Rechte* (Germany's new right), Paderborn: Schöningh, 2011; Andreas Zick and Beate Küpper (eds.), *Wut, Verachtung, Abwertung: Rechtspopulismus in Deutschland* (Anger, contempt, degradation: right-wing populism in Germany), Bonn: Dietz, 2015.

29   For an excellent analysis of the history and strategy of IS, see Will McCants, *The ISIS Apocalypse*, New York: Picador, 2015. The author is also very active on Twitter: @will_mccants.

30   In *The Management of Savagery*, one of the central documents that IS refers to in regard to its ideology and agenda, the author Abu Bakr Naji devotes a whole chapter to the strategy of polarization. The text was translated by Will McCants in 2006 and is recommended reading for anyone who wants to understand the dogmatic foundations of IS terrorism. On the polarization and fragmentation of the West as a goal of IS, see also Jessica Lewis McFate et al., *ISIS Forecast: Ramadan 2016*, Middle East Security Report 30, Washington, DC: Institute for the Study of War, 2016, http://www.understandingwar.org/sites/default/files/ISW%20ISIS%20RAMADAN%20FORECAST%202016%20FINAL.pdf.

31   'Dramatische Szenen: Frau bricht nach Mob-Attacke in Flüchtlingsheim zusammen' (Dramatic scenes: woman collapses in refugee shelter after mob attack), Focus Online, http://www.focus.de/politik/Videos/brauner-mob-in-clausnitz-dramatische-szenen-aus-clausnitz-fluecht-lingsheim-frauen-und-kinder-voellig-verstoert_id_5303116.html.

32   'Eric Garner Video: Unedited Version', YouTube (*New York Daily News*), https://www.youtube.com/watch?v=JpGxagKOkv8 (accessed 21 November 2017).

33   Their names only became known in the course of the subsequent investigation. I use them here to describe more precisely the events that led to Eric Garner's death.

34   There is also an audio recording: 'Eric Garner's Final Words', History Is a Weapon, http://www.hiaw.org/garner.

35   Eric Garner had been arrested several times before, for selling untaxed cigarettes and for possession of marijuana.

36   Fanon, *Black Skin, White Masks*, 93. The original French and Philcox's English translation both spell out the word that I have abbreviated here as 'N.' I abbreviate it because,

as a white writer quoting a Black author, I am setting this term in a different context, and am aware of the shifts in meaning and the possible offences that may result.

37 Especially instructive texts in this regard are Judith Butler, 'Endangered/Endangering: Schematic Racism and White Paranoia', and Robert Gooding-Williams, 'Look, a N.!', both in Robert Gooding-Williams (ed.), *Reading Rodney King, Reading Urban Uprising*, New York and London: Routledge, 1993, 15–22 and 157–77.

38 Scarry, 'The Difficulty of Imagining Other Persons', 279.

39 Factors which contributed to Garner's death, the medical examiner found, included his asthma, heart disease and obesity.

40 Fanon, *Black Skin, White Masks*, 91.

41 Clifford Krauss, 'Clash Over a Football Ends with a Death in Police Custody', *New York Times*, 30 December 1994, http://www.nytimes.com/1994/12/30/ nyregion/clash-over-a-football-ends-with-a-death-in-police-custody.html.

42 Ta-Nehisi Coates, *Between the World and Me*, New York: Spiegel and Grau, 2015, 10.

43 George Yancey describes this experience of fear: 'Black people were not the American "we", but the terrorized other.' Brad Evans, 'The Perils of Being a Black Philosopher', interview with George Yancey, *New York Times*, 18 April 2016, http://opinionator.blogs.nytimes.com/2016/04/18/ the-perils-of-being-a-black-philosopher.

44 Coates, *Between the World and Me*, 103.

45 In Dallas, where five police officers were shot by the Black Afghanistan veteran Micah Johnson, the local police had made efforts to de-escalate tensions for years. See Patrick Bahners, 'Ausgerechnet Dallas' (Dallas of all places), *Frankfurter Allgemeine Zeitung*, 10 July 2016, www.faz.net/aktuell/feuillcton/nach-den-polizisten-morden-ausgerechnet-dallas-14333684.html.

46 I will refrain from listing here all the lesbian women I have been mistaken for to whom I bear no resemblance at all.

47 See also Mari J. Matsuda, Charles R. Lawrence III, Richard Delgado and Kimberle Williams Crenshaw

(eds.), *Words that Wound: Critical Race Theory, Assaultive Speech, and the First Amendment*, Boulder, CO: Westview Press, 1993, 13.
48 Hannah Arendt, 'The Jewish Army – The Beginning of Jewish Politics?', trans. John E. Woods, in Arendt, *The Jewish Writings*, ed. Jerome Kohn and Ron H. Feldman, New York: Schocken, 2007, 137.

2 Homogeneous – Natural – Pure

1 Jacques Derrida, 'Shibboleth: For Paul Celan', trans. Joshua Wilner, in *Word Traces*, ed. Aris Fioretos, Baltimore: Johns Hopkins University Press, 1992, 25.
2 Furthermore, differences in religious practices and beliefs are found not only between religious congregations, but also *within* them. Religion in the modern era is always – regardless of all theological doctrines – *lived* religion, and in the lives of the faithful it is more multifaceted and more versatile, across different generations or different regions, than the respective canonical texts or the respective doctrinal authorities may pretend. In principle, the rule that *no coercion* is permitted applies to religious communities too. That means that, for those born into a congregation whose rules they do not or will not conform to, an *exit option* must be available: that members or their relatives must be able to leave if they cannot or do not believe, if the precepts burden them excessively or infringe their rights as autonomous subjects. Being allowed (or able) to believe and being allowed (or able) not to believe are individual rights (or abilities) that are equally deserving of protection. Admission to a faith and to a religious community must not be coerced.
3 Tzvetan Todorov, *The Conquest of America: The Question of the Other*, New York: Harper and Row, 1984, 146.
4 Before any misunderstanding arises: of course such exclusions can sometimes be authorized by a majority, in referendums or parliamentary elections. But that does not change the fact of their potential illiberal, normatively dubious character. Even democratic decisions

are contained within a legal system and limited by guarantees of human rights. But I will come back to this later.

5 In liberalism, on the other hand, a certain pragmatism is apparent: the people delegates its sovereignty to elected representatives. In Germany, the sovereign power of the people is exercised, according to the constitution, only 'in elections and referendums and through special organs of the executive and the judiciary' (Article 20, paragraph 2). For a reformulation of popular sovereignty using discourse theory to expand the concept of democratic decision-making, see also Jürgen Habermas, *Between Facts and Norms: Contributions to a Discourse Theory of Law and Democracy*, Cambridge: Polity, 1996, 287–328.

6 See 'Das Imaginäre der Republik II: Der Körper der Nation' (The imaginary of the republic, part 2: the body of the nation), in Albrecht Koschorke, Susanne Lüdemann, Thomas Frank and Ethel Matala de Mazza, *Der fiktive Staat: Konstruktionen des politischen Körpers in der Geschichte Europas* (The fictive state: constructions of the body politic in the history of Europe), Frankfurt am Main: Fischer Taschenbuch, 2007, 258–66.

7 For a more thorough discussion of the headscarf issue, see Emcke, *Kollektive Identitäten*, 280–83.

8 Ibid.

9 On the other hand, there are several studies which examine why cultural diversity can be advantageous, not only politically and democratically, but also economically. See Quamrul Ashraf and Oded Galor, 'Cultural Diversity, Geographical Isolation, and the Origin of the Wealth of Nations', Working Paper 17640, Cambridge, MA: National Bureau of Economic Research, 2011, http://www.nber.org/papers/w17640.pdf; and Sophia Kerby and Crosby Burns, 'The Top 10 Economic Facts of Diversity in the Workplace: A Diverse Workforce is Integral to a Strong Economy', Center for American Progress, https://www.americanprogress.org/issues/labor/news/2012/07/12/11900/the-top-10-economic-facts-of-diversity-in-the-workplace.

10   According to Marine Le Pen of the French *Front national*, for example, the 'original', 'true' France is situated before the country's historic accession to the European Union at the latest, and perhaps in de Gaulle's time. France is not France, by that logic, when it is integrated in the EU (or NATO). Mainly, however, Marine Le Pen situates 'real' France in the historical time in which there were no French Muslims. When Le Pen criticizes the cultural and religious diversity of present-day France, she is fond of presuming that there ever was such a thing as a truly homogeneous French nation with a uniform identity – however it may have been defined. That is why Le Pen considers ancestry the critical characteristic for the right to French citizenship – and not birth in French territory, as the law of the Fifth Republic stipulates.

11   Benedict Anderson, *Imagined Communities*, London and New York: Verso, 1991 [1983], 6.

12   'Pegida-Anhänger hetzen gegen Nationalspieler auf Kinderschokolade' (Pegida supporters agitate against national players on Kinder chocolate), Spiegel Online, 24 May 2016, http://www.spiegel.de/panorama/gesell schaft/pegida-anhaenger-hetzen-gegen-nationalspieler-aufkinderschokolade-a-1093985.html.

13   'Forschungsprojekt Diskriminierungen im Alltag: Wahrnehmung von Diskriminierung und Antidiskriminierungspolitik in unserer Gesellschaft' (Research project: discrimination in everyday life; perceptions of discrimination and anti-discrimination policy in our society), *Antidiskriminierungsstelle des Bundes* (German federal anti-discrimination office), http://www.antidiskriminierungsstelle.de/SharedDocs/ Downloads/DE/publikationen/forschungsprojekt_diskri-minierung_im_alltag.pdf?__blob=publicationFile.

14   'Boateng will jeder haben' (Everyone wants Boateng), interview with Alexander Gauland, *Der Spiegel*, 4 June 2016, 37, http://www.spiegel.de/spiegel/print/d-145101317.html.

15   The techniques of exclusion and defamation include not least – I will emphasize it again explicitly in this section – the terms used to designate human beings.

To many people who deal with the issue of exclusion as researchers or as political activists, the debate on language, politics and appropriate, inclusive designations is vitally important. Even supposedly 'self-evident' categories such as 'male or female' pose an ethical and political problem because they merely repeat the attributions and binary divisions that ought to be the object of critical reflection. A number of strategies have been proposed in an attempt to supplant less inclusive linguistic conventions: writing 'she or he', 'she/he', or 's/he' to refer to persons of unknown gender; using 'she' and 'her' to represent all genders, compensating for centuries of generic 'he' and 'him'; using 'they' as a gender-neutral singular pronoun; or using one of several new pronouns invented expressly to make all the intended genders visible: 'ze'/'zem', 'ze'/'hir', 'zhe'/'zhim', and more. What is important to me at this point is to state that the attribute 'masculine' or 'feminine', as used in this text, is not asserted as a simply given, objective fact, but always as a historically and culturally informed form. Who is seen, or who may be treated, as 'male' or 'female' in a given context, for what reason, is the subject of controversy, and that is the topic of this section. I hope the forms and terms I use here will be received as respectful, and at the same time as understandable.

16 My heartfelt thanks to Tucké Royale and Maria Sabine Augstein for their patience in answering my questions, for their openness in confiding personal aspects of their experience to me, and for their well-founded and constructive criticism. I alone am responsible, of course, for any flaws and mistakes in the section that follows.

17 Pertinent studies on the origin of the gendered body include Claudia Honegger, *Die Ordnung der Geschlechter* (The order of the sexes), Frankfurt am Main: Campus, 1991; Thomas Faqueur, *Making Sex: Body and Gender from the Greeks to Freud*, Cambridge, MA: Harvard University Press, 1990; and Barbara Duden, *The Woman Beneath the Skin*, Cambridge, MA: Harvard University Press, 1991. On the idea of gender as a social and cultural

mode of existence, see Andrea Maihofer, *Geschlecht als Existenzweise* (Gender as a mode of existence), Frankfurt am Main: Helmer, 1995.

18   On the question how 'difference can be thought in relation to power and dominance relations', see Nico J. Beger, Sabine Hark, Antke Engel, Corinna Genschel and Eva Schäfer (eds.), *Queering Demokratie* (Queering democracy), Berlin: Querverlag, 2000.

19   For the second version, see Stefan Hirschauer, *Die soziale Konstruktion der Transsexualität: Über die Medizin und den Geschlechtswechsel* (The social construction of transsexuality: on medicine and sex change), Frankfurt am Main: Suhrkamp, 2015 [1993].

20   To describe it more precisely, and perhaps more surprisingly: in fact, there are also transgender persons who do not feel the sexual characteristics they were born with are 'wrong' or 'conflicting'. They may find them beautiful and fitting. But what does not fit them is the interpretation of those characteristics as 'definitely female' or 'definitely male'.

21   See also Andrea Allerkamp, *Anruf, Adresse, Appell: Figuration der Kommunikation in Philosophie und Literatur* (Invocation, address, appeal: the figuration of communication in philosophy and literature), Bielefeld: Transcript, 2005, 31–41.

22   Matsuda et al. (eds.), *Words that Wound*, 5.

23   'To be injured by speech is to suffer a loss of context, that is, not to know where you are.' Judith Butler, *Excitable Speech: A Politics of the Performative*, New York and Abingdon: Routledge, 1997, 4.

24   The figures are quoted in Jacqueline Rose, 'Who Do You Think You Are?', *London Review of Books*, 2 May 2016, https://www.lrb.co.uk/v38/n09/jacqueline-rose/who-do-you-think-you-are.

25   'Packers' are various kinds of penis prostheses. 'Binders' are worn to flatten the breasts, making them less outwardly visible. Thanks to Laura Merkt, who shared her knowledge both generously and humorously.

26   The desire to adjust one's officially recognized gender or one's body to one's internal convictions has nothing to

do with sexual orientation, by the way. Transsexuality, as the writer and activist Jennifer Pinney Boylan once described it, 'is not about who you want to go to bed *with*, it's who you want to go to bed *as*'. Quoted in Rose, 'Who Do You Think You Are?'

27 Paul B. Preciado, *Testo Junkie: Sex, Drugs and Biopolitics in the Pharmacopornographic Era*, trans. Bruce Benderson, New York: Feminist Press, 2013, 56.

28 Ibid., 143.

29 See the article by Julian Carter, 'Transition', in *Postposttranssexual: Key Concepts for a Twenty-first-century Transgender Studies*, TSQ 1:1–2, 2014, 235ff.

30 Preciado, *Testo Junkie*, 66.

31 Ibid., 55–6.

32 The text of the law (in German) can be found at: http://www.gesetze-im-internet.de/tsg/BJNR016540980.html.

33 Ibid. There is a further condition: records may be changed when 'it can be assumed with high probability that the person's feeling of belonging to the other sex will not change'.

34 From the ruling of the First Senate of the German Federal Constitutional Court, 11 January 2001, https://www.bundesverfassungsgericht.de/entscheidungen/rs20110111_1bvr329507.html.

35 For a critical discussion of the pathologization of transgender persons, see Diana Demiel, 'Was bedeuten DSM-IV und ICD-10?' (What do DSM-IV and ICD-10 mean?), in Anne Allex (ed.), *Stop Trans*Pathologisierung* (Stop trans*pathologization), Neu-Ulm: AG SPAK, 2014, 43–51.

36 Daniel Mendelsohn, *The Elusive Embrace: Desire and the Riddle of Identity*, New York: Vintage, 2000, 25.

37 The new-right discourse in particular demands unequivocal gender. 'Gender functions in this context as a social usher in the strictly anti-individualistic, authoritarian and hierarchical construction of the "national community" [*Volksgemeinschaft*]. Conceptions of masculinity (or masculinities) and femininity (femininities) have a function for the inner cohesion of the community.' Juliane Lang, 'Familie und Vaterland in der Krise: Der

extrem rechte Diskurs um Gender' (Family and fatherland in crisis: the far-right discourse on gender), in Sabine Hark and Paula-Irene Villa (eds.), *Anti-Genderismus: Sexualität und Geschlecht als Schauplätze aktueller politischer Auseinandersetzungen* (Anti-genderism: sexuality and gender as domains of current political disputes), Bielefeld: Transcript, 2015, 169.

38   Oddly enough, trans persons themselves have to pay for the psychiatric evaluations required by the court. Hormone therapy, on the other hand, is paid for by health insurance once the experts have certified the diagnosis of 'transsexualism'. There would appear to be a contradiction here: Ultimately, the legislation treats 'transsexualism' as a disease. But in that case, the diagnosis required by the court ought to be covered by health insurance.

39   On the lack of sensitivity to violence against gender-nonconforming persons, see Ines Pohlkamp, *Genderbashing: Diskriminierung und Gewalt an den Grenzen der Zweigeschlechtlichkeit* (Gender bashing: discrimination and violence on the boundaries of binary gender), Münster: Unrast, 2014.

40   See also Carolin Emcke, 'Orlando', *Süddeusche Zeitung*, 17 June 2016, http://www.sueddeutsche.de/politik/kolumne-orlando-1.3038967.

41   Eribon, *Returning to Reims*, 215.

42   'Germany', in *OSCE ODIHR Hate Crime Reporting*, http://hatecrime.osce.org/germany?year=2014.

43   In describing violence against trans persons, it is also important to reflect on the particular danger that trans people of colour face. Transphobia and racism form a cruel alliance, and the double vulnerability should not be overlooked. The seven trans women who were murdered in the United States in the first seven weeks of 2013 were all people of colour. Their particular defencelessness often involves the fact that many people of colour are especially marginalized, cannot find a job and are consequently compelled to do sex work. The deprivation of rights that accompanies this situation puts them at risk of the most brutal violence.

44 Violence against trans persons is often 'justified' by the explanation that the trans person 'deceived' the perpetrator about their sex. In this way the victim of violence is also blamed for the violence. On this pattern of justification of transphobic violence, see Talia Mae Bettcher, 'Evil Deceivers and Make-Believers', in Susan Stryker and Aren Z. Aizura (eds.), *The Transgender Studies Reader*, vol. 2, New York: Routledge, 2013, 278–90.

45 'Transgender: Toilettenstreit in den USA auf neuem Höhepunkt' (Transgender: toilets conflict in the US reaches new crisis), Deutsche Welle, http://www. dw.com/de/transgender-toilettenstreit-in-usa-auf-neuem-höhepunkt/a-19283386.

46 '"Do You See How Much I'm Suffering Here?"': Abuse Against Transgender Women in US Immigration Detention', Human Rights Watch, 23 March 2016, https://www.hrw.org/report/2016/03/23/do-you-see-how-much-im-suffering-here/abuse-against-transgender-women-us.

47 If a person wants a medical gender adaptation procedure, on the other hand, an expert report would be appropriate – if only for health insurance purposes. But this is a controversial question: some people consider the idea of pathologization unacceptable, while others find the issue of economic costs more important.

48 Mendelsohn, *The Elusive Embrace*, 26–7.

49 There has been speculation that that was the reason why the Bataclan was chosen as the site of an attack. 'Pourquoi le Bataclan est-il régulièrement visé?' (Why is the Bataclan regularly targeted?), *Le point*, 14 November 2015, http://www.lepoint.fr/societe/le-bataclan-une-cible-regulierement-visee-14-11-2015-1981544_23.php.

50 Although of course we do not know whether their desire is really homosexual, or whether that is merely attributed to them.

51 William McCants, 'How Terrorists Kill', *Time*, 10 December 2015, http://time.com/4144457/how-terrorists-kill.

52 Cf. Katajun Amirpur, '"Islam gleich Gewalt": Der fatale Gleichklang von Kriegern und Kritikern' ('Islam equals

violence': the fatal unison of warriors and critics), *Blätter für deutsche und internationale Politik*, January 2015, https://www.blaetter.de/archiv/jahrgaenge/2015/januar/»islam-gleich-gewalt«.

53 This book will have little to say about political strategies of imagery. For more on that, see my text (in German) on the James Foley video, Carolin Emcke, 'Dankrede' (Acceptance speech), *Deutsche Akademie für Sprache und Dichtung* (German academy of language and literature), http://www.deutscheakademie.de/de/ausze-ichnungen/johann-heinrich-merck-preis/carolin-emcke/dankrede.

54 Quoted in Eric Schmitt, 'In Battle to Defang ISIS, U.S. Targets Its Psychology', *New York Times*, 28 December 2014, https://www.nytimes.com/2014/12/29/us/politics/in-battle-to-defang-isis-us-targets-its-psychology-.html.

55 Pieter van Ostaeyen has archived English translations of Al-Adnani's statements online: https://pietervanos-taeyen.com/category/al-adnani-2.

56 On the role of al-Zarqawi, see Yassin Musharbash, *Die neue al-Qaida: Innenansichten eines lernenden Terror-Netzwerks*, Cologne: Kiepenheuer & Witsch, 2007, 54–61.

57 The link is given here only for documentation, not as a recommendation. The link is to a page with an explicit warning that the video is IS propaganda and unsuitable for young viewers. It contains violence and commends the IS terror regime. 'New ISIS Video: Upon the Prophetic Methodology', LiveLeak, http://www.liveleak.com/view?i=181_1406666485.

58 Abu Bakr Al-Baghdadi, 'A Message to the Mujahidin and the Muslim Ummah in the Month of Ramadan', https://archive.org/details/AMessageToThe MujahidinAndTheMuslimUmmahInTheMonth OfRamadan. The version at archive.org has the Arabic *khilāfah* for 'caliphate'.

59 One IS propaganda film is explicitly devoted to this issue: the 12-minute video *Breaking the Borders*. There is an interesting controversy as to whether IS actually succeeded in forming a proto-state

structure. See Daphné Richemond-Barak and Daniel J. Schulster, 'Why ISIS Does Not Weaken Our World Order', https://www.ict.org.il/Article/1522/ Why-ISIS-Does-Not-Weaken-Our-World-Order.

60   Abu Bakr al-Baghdadi, 'Wa-ya'ba 'llah illa an yutimm nurahu', quoted in Cole Bunzel, *From Paper State to Caliphate: The Ideology of the Islamic State*, Center for Middle East Policy at the Brookings Institution, https:// www.brookings.edu/wp-content/uploads/2016/06/ The-ideology-of-the-Islamic-State.pdf.

61   Fawaz A. Gerges writes that 30 per cent of the top leadership level of the IS's military wing consists of former Iraqi army or police officers who lost their positions in the course of the Americans' de-Ba'athification program. Fawaz A. Gerges, *ISIS: A History*, Princeton, NJ: Princeton University Press, 2016, 149. See also Malise Ruthven's review of Gerges's book, 'How to Understand ISIS', *New York Review of Books*, 23 June 2016, http://www.nybooks.com/articles/2016/06/23/how-to-understand-isis.

62   Al-Baghdadi, 'A Message to the Mujahidin'.

63   On IS's special conception of temporality, see Yassin Musharbash's 'beginners' course in jihadist ideology': 'Wie tickt der IS?' (How does IS tick?), part 1, Zeit Online, http://blog.zeit.de/radikale-ansichten/2015/03/30/ wie-tickt-der-1.

64   Just as Muslim scholars all over the world oppose IS's distortion of Islam, many Sunni tribes in Iraq and Syria refuse allegiance to the IS. Al-Baghdadi seems to have underestimated the complex political and social reality, both abroad and in his own territory. Fawaz A. Gerges, 'The Three Manifestos That Paved the Way for Islamic State', *Los Angeles Times*, 15 April 2016, http://www. latimes.com/opinion/op-ed/la-oe-0417-gerges-islamic-state-theorists-20160417-story.html.

65   Mary Douglas, *Purity and Danger: An Analysis of Concepts of Pollution and Taboo*, London and New York: Routledge, 2003 [1966], 4.

66   Ben Tufft, 'Isis "Executes up to 200 Fighters" for Trying to Flee Jihad and Return Home', *Independent*, 29

December 2014, http://www.independent.co.uk/news/
world/middle-east/isis-executes-at-least-120-fighters-for-
trying-to-flee-and-go-home-9947805.html.

67 Abu Bakr Naji, *The Management of Savagery: The
Most Critical Stage Through Which the Umma will
Pass*, trans. William McCants, John M. Olin Institute
for Strategic Studies at Harvard University, 2006,
https://azelin.files.wordpress.com/2010/08/abu-
bakr-naji-the-management-of-savagery-the-most-
critical-stage-through-which-the-umma-will-pass.pdf,
14.

68 A psychoanalytical interpretation might discern an 'anal
fixation' in this cult of purity, the extreme obsession
with order and the fear of loss of control. On connections between populism and notions of purity – apart
from IS – see Robert Pfaller, *Das schmutzige Heilige und
die reine Vernunft: Symptome der Gegenwartskultur*
(The pollution of the sacred and the purity of reason),
Frankfurt am Main: S. Fischer, 2008, 180–95.

69 Naji, *The Management of Savagery*, 72.

70 The quotation is from the English translation of Abu
Omar al-Baghdadi's speech 'Say I Am on Clear Proof from
My Lord', https://pietervanostaeyen.files.wordpress.
com/2014/12/say_i_am_on_clear_proof_from_my_lord-
englishwww-islamicline-com.pdf, 6 (at 'Seventh').

71 Rachel Avraham, 'ISIS Warns Refugees: "Don't
Flee to Europe"', JerusalemOnline, 18 September
2015, http://www.jerusalemonline.com/news/world-
news/around-the-globe/isis-warns-refugees-dont-
flee-to-europe-15954.

3 In Praise of the Impure

1 'Fanatisme', in *Encyclopédie de Diderot et d'Alembert:
lettre F (Encyclopédie, ou Dictionnaire raisonné des
sciences, des arts et des métiers)*, La Bibliothèque des
classiques, 2018 [1751–72].

2 Aleida Assmann, 'Ähnlichkeit als Performanz: Ein neuer
Zugang zu Identitätskonstruktionen und Empathie-
Regimen' (Similarity as performance: a new approach to
constructions of identity and regimes of empathy), in Anil

Bhati and Dorothee Kimmich (eds.), *Ähnlichkeit: Ein kulturtheoretisches Paradigma* (Similarity: a paradigm of cultural theory), Constance: Konstanz University Press, 2015, 171.

3   Hannah Arendt, *The Human Condition*, Chicago: University of Chicago Press, 1998 [1958], 4.

4   Ibid., 8.

5   Jean-Luc Nancy, 'Being Singular Plural', in *Being Singular Plural*, trans. Robert D. Richardson and Anne E. O'Byrne, Palo Alto: Stanford University Press, 2000, 32.

6   Ingeborg Bachmann, 'Frankfurter Vorlesungen' (Frankfurt lectures), in Ingeborg Bachmann, *Werke* (Works), vol. 4, Munich: Piper, 1993, 192–3.

7   Martin Saar, *Die Immanenz der Macht: Politische Theorie nach Spinoza* (The immanence of power: political theory after Spinoza), Berlin: Suhrkamp, 2013, 395.

8   'Blickveränderungen' (Changes of perspective), *Lettre International*, 109, Summer 2015.

9   I have written on the special challenge of remembering the Shoah in the present in my column (Carolin Emcke, 'Erinnern' [Remembering], *Süddeutsche Zeitung*, 29 January 2016, http://www.sueddeutsche.de/politik/kolumne-erinnern-1.2840316), and at more length in Carolin Emcke, *Weil es sagbar ist: Zeugenschaft und Gerechtigkeit* (Because it is sayable: witness and justice), Frankfurt am Main: S. Fischer, 2013.

10 That is perhaps because international literature is mainly expected to be read in the original, and is therefore relegated to foreign-language courses. In this regard, it might make more sense to establish a separate subject for international cultural history or world literature.

11 Michel Foucault, '12 January 1983', *The Government of Self and Others: Lectures at the Collège de France*, trans. Graham Burchell, Basingstoke: Palgrave Macmillan, 2010, 41–74.

12 Ibid., 50.

13 Eva Illouz, *Israel*, trans. Michael Adrian, Berlin: Suhrkamp, 2013, 7–8.

14 Albrecht Koschorke, *Fact and Fiction: Elements of a General Theory of Narrative*, Berlin: de Gruyter, 2018.

15 The 'Hate Poetry Slam' is a contemporary creative
    intervention that fills truth-telling against hatred and
    fanaticism with humour and irony. It was founded and
    developed by Ebru Taşdemir, Doris Akrap, Deniz Yücel,
    Mely Kiyak and Yassin Musharbash – later joined
    by Özlem Gezer, Özlem Topçu, Hasnain Kazim and
    Mohamed Amjahid. In this programme, performed for
    live audiences in clubs or theatres, the journalists read a
    selection of the most rabid hate mail they have received
    from readers. The letters are addressed to the journalists
    personally, and lavish them with an outpouring of
    racist and sexist insults. They insult and vilify (often
    in shockingly bad grammar, incidentally); they scold
    and gripe with arrogant superiority and islamophobic
    hatred. In the 'Hate Poetry' format, the recipients of
    these letters read them out loud, bringing them out of
    the silence of the editorial offices onto the stage, and in
    the process freeing themselves from the helplessness and
    melancholy that ordinarily afflict everyone who receives
    such mail. By making this hate mail public, they break
    open the one-to-one relationship that a letter, even the
    most disgusting one, imposes between the sender and
    the recipient. They refuse to bear this hatred alone.
    Nor do they want to tolerate it in silence. They want to
    call the public as witnesses, as an audience; they want
    to break out of their role as defenceless recipients of
    hatred and perform an ironic reading that exposes and
    subverts the racism to which they are subjected. The
    participants in 'Hate Poetry' have brought off a clever
    and funny reversal of subject and object: the object
    of laughter, of ridicule, is no longer the journalists'
    supposed background, their supposed identity, their
    religion, their appearance – but the texts of hatred. And
    they manage this without exposing the authors of the
    letters. They do not rage against a nationalistic, racist
    'mob'; they laugh at what people say and do. They
    process it and transform it through ironic dissidence.
    And so 'Hate Poetry' is not only a reading, but also a
    party, a celebration: the journalists hold a contest for
    the most repulsive readers' letters in categories such as

'Dear Ms C...', Dear Mr A...', 'Cancel My Subscription', 'Grand Opera' and 'Quick and Dirty'. The audience get to vote for the winners. This is a tricky business, because the humour on stage makes the audience laugh at texts and terms that are not funny, only repulsive. The raw racism, islamophobia, sexism and misanthropy that can be heard are mortifying and shocking. For the audience, the force of the verbal injury initially hits everyone – and every spectator in the house asks themselves: How does that feel? Could that be said to me? Why not? What position do I have here: that of a spectator, someone these letters are not aimed at? Every spectator must ask: How do I respond to this language, to this hatred? What does it mean to laugh about it? What might be an appropriate reaction? With its creative resistance, the format not only makes laughter contagious in the audience, but also provokes serious reflection on day-to-day racism, on the spectator's own social position and the question of necessary supportive alliances.

16 Arendt, *The Human Condition*, 200.